simply
stations

writing

· grades k–4 ·

For information:

Corwin
A SAGE Company
2455 Teller Road
Thousand Oaks, California 91320
(800) 233–9936
www.corwin.com

SAGE Publications Ltd.
1 Oliver's Yard
55 City Road
London EC1Y 1SP
United Kingdom

SAGE Publications India Pvt. Ltd.
B 1/I 1 Mohan Cooperative Industrial Area
Mathura Road, New Delhi 110 044
India

SAGE Publications Asia-Pacific Pte. Ltd.
18 Cross Street #10–10/11/12
China Square Central
Singapore 048423

Senior Acquisitions Editor: Tori Bachman

Editorial Development Manager: Julie Nemer

Associate Content Development
  Editor: Sharon Wu

Production Editor: Melanie Birdsall

Copy Editor: Heather Kerrigan

Typesetter: Integra

Proofreader: Susan Schon

Cover and Interior Designer: Gail Buschman

Marketing Manager: Deena Meyer

Icon sources: Time-Saving Tip: davooda/Shutterstock.com; EL Tip: iStock.com/ilyaliren

Station icon sources: Listening and Speaking: iStock.com/ilyaliren; Independent Reading: iStock.com/ilyaliren; Partner Reading: iStock.com/ilyaliren; Writing: iStock.com/da-vooda; Poetry: iStock.com/GreenTana; Drama: iStock.com/GreenTana; Word Study: iStock.com/ilyaliren; Inquiry and Research: iStock.com/GreenTana; Let's Talk: iStock.com/ilyaliren; Letter Writing: iStock.com/bubaone

Library of Congress Cataloging-in-Publication Data

Names: Diller, Debbie, author.
Title: Simply stations : writing, grades K–4 / Debbie Diller.
Description: Thousand Oaks, California : Corwin, [2021]
Identifiers: LCCN 2020036733 | ISBN 9781544395005 (paperback) | ISBN 9781071838686 (adobe pdf)
Subjects: LCSH: English language—Composition and exercises—Study and teaching (Elementary) | Classroom learning centers. | Group work in education.
Classification: LCC LB1576 .D46475 2021 | DDC 372.6/044—dc23
LC record available at https://lccn.loc.gov/2020036733

Printed in the United States of America

This book is printed on acid-free paper.

21 22 23 24 25 10 9 8 7 6 5 4 3 2 1

simply stations

writing

[
• grades k–4 •

planning tools

launching lessons

printables
]

resources.corwin.com/simplystations-writing

debbie diller

CORWIN Literacy

Contents

Visit the companion website at
resources.corwin.com/simplystations-writing
for downloadable resources.

Literacy Stations Overview

You may already have well-established independent reading routines in your classroom. Perhaps your students work with partners at several reading-related stations, such as an Independent Reading or Partner Reading stations. But now you're wondering how to help kids write just as well as they read.

A **Writing station** can be a place of joy for students, a time they look forward to writing all kinds of things—greeting cards, stories, information booklets, and news articles! In this book, you'll find many ideas for how to build on what you teach during whole group and independent writing time to establish a successful Writing station. As you model writing in front of your students, they then practice those same things during independent writing *and* at the Writing station. Students that have supported opportunities to choose ideas, write about what they know and care about, and share with an audience daily will become stronger writers. The Writing station can be part of this practice.

Photo by Nick McIntosh

#simplystations

@debbie.diller
(Instagram)

https://www
.facebook.com/
dillerdebbie
(Facebook)

@debbiediller
(Twitter)

www.debbiediller
.com
(website)

Just like the other books in the Simply Stations series, this one includes ideas for easy setup and maintenance, as well as suggestions for keeping the Writing station interesting all year long. You'll find everything you need to get started in the pages that follow: tools and materials that motivate kids to write; sample lessons for introducing and adding depth to the writing children do at this station; and resources to help them write independently of you. I've also shared ideas for how to plan with timeless standards, such as choosing topics and composing well-crafted narrative, informational, and opinion pieces, that can be taught and then transferred as students practice these now-familiar skills with a partner at the Writing station.

This book is dedicated to helping you implement this powerful station in a simple yet meaningful way. I'd love to see and hear your ideas on the Writing station, too, so please check in with me on social media using the hashtag #simplystations.

With purposeful practice in mind,
Debbie

Literacy Stations Basics

What Is a Literacy Station?

A literacy station is a small, defined space (portable or stationary) where students **practice** with a **partner**. Students work together using **familiar** materials and tasks they can do to practice reading, writing, listening, speaking, and/or working with words. The children use previously taught academic vocabulary as they engage in **meaningful work** that has been modeled previously in whole or small group instruction.

The Writing station is a space equipped with resources you've modeled with previously, so students can write without your help there. You'll just need a small table near a bulletin board or wall space where you can place materials related to writing after you've taught with them. Some teachers choose to duplicate the Writing station by having a space where pairs of kids write fiction and another small place where another pair of students practice writing informational text. Kids may discuss what they will write about before writing, they may write together, or they may choose to write alone but share what they're writing with their partner.

How Do Literacy Stations Fit Into the Literacy Block?

In a classroom where Reading and Writing Workshop takes place, the literacy block is broken into segments: whole class lessons for modeling, small group instruction, and stations work time. Stations work happens simultaneous to small group instruction during reading time. As the teacher meets with a small group, the rest of the class works in pairs reading and writing at **literacy stations** around the classroom. Literacy stations provide purposeful practice.

Around the classroom, pairs of students work together at a variety of stations, including an Independent Reading station (or two), a Listening and Speaking station (or two), a Writing station, two Partner Reading stations, a Word Study station, and a Poetry station. Two children are using retelling pieces and a familiar book at a Drama station; several students are engaged in asking and answering questions at the Inquiry and Research station; and two scholars are talking about a fine art print at the Let's Talk station. (For more information on each station, please see the related title in the Simply Stations series.)

Some stations, such as the Writing station, may be duplicated. At the Writing station, two students sit at a small table writing about topics they've chosen.

EL TIP: Conversation cards have sentence stems to help your multilingual learners respond orally to what they've read. (There are printable conversation cards at **resources .corwin.com/simply stations-writing**.)

They may spend a few minutes talking with their partner about what they plan to do as a writer today (come up with an idea for a new piece, reread and revise a piece from Writing Workshop, check for punctuation and spelling with a peer). In another Writing station, two other children choose a piece of writing they started in Writing Workshop from their writing folders and continue to work on those. They are seated at a table while others sit on stools by the countertop. At both Writing stations, all materials needed are at students' fingertips. After they write a bit, partners may share what they wrote with each other. They help each other improve their writing by listening and asking questions.

Each station has been carefully introduced, one at a time, over the first month of school. Students know what is expected of them, they have everything they need, and they are working on tasks they *can* do successfully. In every book of the Simply Stations series, you'll find suggestions for how to set up and introduce a station.

During the first few weeks of school while children are learning to work at stations, the teacher circulates freely around the classroom facilitating, listening in on students, and talking with them about what they are learning. Once children demonstrate independence with classroom routines for literacy stations (usually about four to six weeks into the school year), the teacher begins to work with small groups. A management board is used to help children move independently to several stations daily. Everything you need for your management board can be found on pages 18–21 of this book!

What Is the Ideal Number of Students at Each Station?

I recommend having children work in pairs (yes, just two kids!) at each station. This increases student engagement and reduces classroom noise if you space children thoughtfully around the room. You will need more stations, but they will be easier to maintain because you don't have to change things out as often. Use the easy-to-follow directions throughout this series for how to introduce each station to ensure success for you and your students.

How Do I Determine Partnerships?

At the start of the year, think about who gets along well and pair those children together. Once you begin small groups, try pairing students from the same flexible reading group. That way they won't lose their partners when you meet with a group. Also, you'll find that if you plan for things children *can* do, they will push each other further if paired with someone at about the same reading level. If you have an odd number of children, you might have a group of three students work at the Writing station. Because they might be writing alone, there is enough for three kids to do here without distracting each other. Nonetheless, be sure the three get along well together if you partner them!

TIME-SAVING TIP: If you establish stations well during your first few weeks with your students, you will save time in the long run (even if you are taking over a class partway through the school year). Get to know your students, so you'll be ready to start small groups as soon as possible. Building relationships and routines is a valuable use of time.

How Long Do Students Work at Each Station?

Each literacy station lasts about twenty minutes in Grades 1–4. In kindergarten, children may spend about fifteen minutes per station. Typically, students go to two rotations back-to-back while the teacher meets with two small groups. If you decide to meet with three groups a day, you might have a whole group lesson after two rounds of stations and then meet with a third small group while all students do independent reading or go to a third round of literacy stations.

How Do Literacy Stations Fit Into the Day?

Literacy stations are just one component in a balanced literacy or a workshop approach to teaching reading and writing. Several sample schedules follow from primary and intermediate classrooms to show where stations fit in the day. Be flexible and create a schedule that works for you.

SAMPLE PRIMARY SCHEDULE for LITERACY

8:00–8:10	Morning Meeting (community building time)
8:10–8:25	Whole Group Lesson for Modeling Using Interactive Read Aloud
8:25–8:45	Literacy Stations and Small Group (round one)
8:45–9:05	Literacy Stations and Small Group (round two)
9:05–9:15	Reflection Time for Stations and Small Group
9:15–9:20	Brain Break
9:20–9:35	Whole Group Lesson for Modeling Using Shared Reading and Word Study
9:35–9:55	Whole Class Independent Reading Time (teacher confers 1:1 or may meet with a third small group)
9:55–10:05	Whole Group Lesson for Modeling Writing
10:05–10:30	Whole Class Independent Writing Time (teacher confers with students 1:1 or may meet with a small group for writing)
10:30–10:40	Sharing/Reflection Time for Writing

SAMPLE INTERMEDIATE SCHEDULE for LITERACY

8:00–8:10	Morning Meeting (community building time; students do book talks/share what they're reading)
8:10–8:25	Whole Group Lesson for Modeling Using Interactive Read Aloud or Shared Reading Integrating Word Study/Vocabulary
8:25–8:45	Whole Class Independent Reading Time (teacher confers 1:1 or may meet with a small group for reading)
8:45–9:05	Literacy Stations, Book Clubs, and Small Group (some teachers do another twenty-minute round of stations if schedules allow)
9:05–9:15	Whole Group Lesson for Modeling Writing
9:15–9:40	Whole Class Independent Writing Time (teacher confers with students 1:1 or may meet with a small group for writing)
9:40–9:50	Reflection Time for Reading and Writing

How Long Is It Going to Take Me to Prepare for These Stations?

I've included time-saving tips in each book to help ease preparation. The most important thing to remember is to take what you're teaching and *transfer those materials and tasks* to each literacy station. Don't make a bunch of stuff just for stations!

How Often Should the Teacher Change Things at a Station?

Stations are not changed out weekly but involve **spiral reviews** with young scholars returning to work multiple times over several weeks with the same materials and tasks. It's okay for children to write narratives (or informational text) week after week at the Writing station, but give them options so they might write something different if they'd like. Let them make stuff, such as books, postcards, or directions, at this station, and you'll see them sticking with a piece of writing for several sessions. This is the work of an authentic writer. (I worked on this book many, many days in a row!)

Spiral review means that students keep practicing things multiple times throughout the year. For example, if you've been teaching children about choosing topics they're interested in, students can keep practicing this all year long at the Writing station. You don't have to have kids just do this the week you've taught it. When students become familiar with how to choose a writing idea, it will be easier for them to transfer what they're learning to new compositions as they use a heart map or browse through photos or look at model texts at the Writing station—just like they did in Writing Workshop.

In Section 3 of this book, I'll show you how to teach and then have children practice for transfer at the Writing station using what you've already taught. (No need to constantly create new stations materials!)

Simply change out the genres students choose to write from (e.g., list, letter, card, story, fractured folktale, informational text, poem) and what they might try as writers (author's craft, such as adding details, variety of punctuation, different sentence lengths) over time. Be intentional with your changes. Pay attention to student interests and what they're learning to do as writers. Ask for children's input when possible.

Why Are Literacy Stations Effective?

- This is **meaningful** work for the rest of the class during small group time.

- Children like to **talk** and to work with their **peers**. Enjoyment increases engagement!

- **Partner practice** helps students become **independent of the teacher**. Kids aren't working alone. They practice *with* a partner, doing tasks together.

- **Choice** and **student ownership** promote independence. At the Writing station, students should have a choice of what they write about, the materials they use, and the genre they use. Provide writing samples and supports, but give kids choices! Watch, listen, and be open to the kinds of things your students *like* to write!

- **Transfer of learning** occurs as scholars work with familiar tasks and materials previously modeled by the teacher. Discuss what you'll add to the Writing station as a result of what they've been learning to do as writers. For example, if you are reading books with dialogue in speech bubbles and notice kids want to give this a try, add blank speech bubbles (or a bubble pattern to trace). Or, if a student is ill and classmates want to create get well cards, model how to do this and add cardmaking materials.

Two students work at a Writing station.

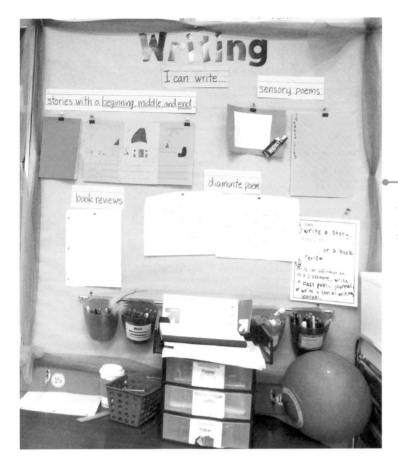

Class-made writing samples are displayed in the Writing station as reminders of what students might write.

This class has a Fiction Writing station and another Nonfiction Writing station on the countertop by the windows.

Getting Started
With Stations

Do you feel overwhelmed about all your students working with partners around the room? Creating a plan for setting up stations and introducing them to your class, one station at a time, will help both you and your students experience success.

Plan for Physical Space

1 Make a list of stations you'd like to have in your classroom. Begin with the end in mind. If you list stations you might want to have for the year, it will help you when planning for space.

You'll want to include some stationary stations and others that are portable to utilize every inch of space in your classroom. A sample list follows, and includes space for you to make your own list. You might label stationary stations with an "S" and portable ones with a "P," as shown. Remember that you can duplicate a station, too! You'll want enough for everyone to partner up. And, yes, if you have twenty-two kids, plan for eleven small spaces around the room. (Don't worry—I'll show you how to introduce each station, one at a time!)

SAMPLE LIST of LITERACY STATIONS	LITERACY STATIONS I PLAN to SET UP
• Writing station – S	
• Listening and Speaking station – P	
• Independent Reading station – S/P	
• Partner Reading station – S/P	
• Poetry station – S	
• Drama station – P	
• Word Study station – S/P	
• Inquiry and Research station – S	
• Let's Talk station – P	

2 Create a classroom map of your space using chart paper and sticky notes with a colleague. If you work together, you can help each other decide if there are things in your space that could move or be eliminated. And you may be able to use similar designs in neighboring classrooms!

  a. Draw in permanent fixtures like windows, doors, closets, technology, etc. on the perimeter of your paper. (Don't draw desks or tables yet. Save them until the end.)

  b. Using sticky notes, plan for where to place your whole group and small group teaching areas. Don't put them on top of each other! Balance these big spaces. Make a sticky note for your classroom library, too, and use this space as a focal point. This will become your Independent Reading station during stations time and a place for students to choose books for other independent reading times.

  c. Using additional sticky notes, label each with a station you'd like to have. Use the list you created in step 1. Think about which may be portable, like the Listening and Speaking station or a Partner Reading station, and which may be stationary, like the Writing station placed near a bulletin board or wall space. Place these sticky notes around the perimeter first and then fill in interior spaces. To minimize noise and distractions, decide how to space out your stations, so they aren't on top of each other.

TIME-SAVING TIP: Planning for where to place stations before starting them will save tons of time! This creates a structure for where students will work that adds time on task for kids. They can get right to work when they know where to go and what to do there. It will also cut down on noise and disruption, because children will be spaced around the room.

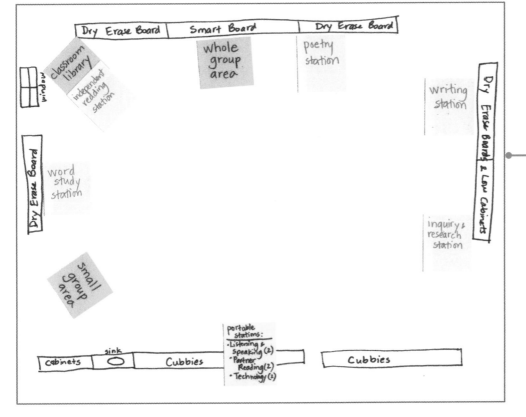

Classroom map made with a colleague. First we placed yellow sticky notes to show the largest areas. Then we added pink sticky notes to show stationary stations. We ended with a blue sticky note listing portable stations that will be taken to desks in the middle of the room.

d. Move around sticky notes until you have a workable plan, keeping flexibility in mind. Be open to changing things if the flow doesn't work.

e. Work with your colleague to place furniture in your classroom using your map. Place desks and tables *last, not first*. They will fit! It's like a puzzle. Place the perimeter pieces first, and then fill in the middle of your classroom.

f. Don't try to make every piece of furniture fit if it doesn't work. Most classrooms have more "stuff" than is needed. Be sure to leave space for children.

MY CLASSROOM MAP

Make a Stations Roll-Out Plan

3 Plan to introduce one station at a time. Think about what your students need to practice and what they *can* do early in the year. Start slowly and simply. Which will you introduce first, second, and so on?

I have found over the years that introducing Independent Reading, followed by Partner Reading and then Listening and Speaking, offers the smoothest modeling, learning, and practicing. Then introduce additional stations according to your students' needs and your curriculum and standards. I have noticed that kids are more successful at the Writing station when Writing Workshop is already established in the classroom. That way students can practice what you're expecting them to do as writers at the Writing station, too.

OUR BEGINNING-of-the-YEAR STATIONS	OUR BEGINNING-of-the-YEAR STATIONS
1. Independent Reading station 2. Partner Reading station 3. Listening and Speaking station	1. _____ 2. _____ 3. _____

See Section 2 of each book in the Simply Stations series for Launch Lessons for each specific station. You'll also find an accompanying Checklist of Routines to Model and Expect for the station.

Model and explain your expectations. Then have all students try the station in your whole group area, so you can monitor and assist. Do this for several days with one station until you're sure students will be able to do this independently of you.

4 Once your students seem to be doing the first station independently, introduce the next station. Follow step 2 again for this station.

Introduce Independent Reading to the whole class at their seats.

On another day, introduce Partner Reading to the whole class around the carpet perimeter.

5 When students are showing independence with two stations, try having half the class do the first station and the other half do this new one.

In a few days, have half the class do the Independent Reading station while the other half works at a Partner Reading station.

6 Continue to layer on one station at a time, in this way, until you have enough stations for students to work in pairs. There is no perfect number of stations. Do what works best for your children and you. When your students know how to do three or four stations well, introduce the management board. See pages 18–21 in this section for how to create and introduce a management board.

7 Once students can use the management board to work in their stations independently of you, layer on meeting with small groups. The foundational process leading to this step usually takes about four to six weeks in most classrooms. Add the Meet With Teacher icon to your management board. Again, see page 18 of this section on Literacy Station Management Board How-To.

Start small group teaching when students can work independently of you.

8 Add new stations, one at a time, as you teach with new standards and change out materials as students show you they are ready.

Use the planning tool and roll-out calendar found in Section 4 (see printables on the companion website) to help you plan for when and how you might introduce each new station.

Take your time introducing each station thoughtfully. Be sure students understand your expectations and *can* do what you want them to do at that station before moving on to the next one. Your investment in time will pay off.

Are There Special Considerations for Kindergarten Rollout?

In kindergarten, follow the above plan but start the first week of school with placeholders for stations. Think about what your children can do independent of the teacher at their tables, and introduce one activity for each table group. Possibilities include partner playdough, partner puzzles, dry erase supplies for tracing, reading easy books from a basket on the table by talking about the pictures, or drawing pictures on plain white paper with colored pencils.

Sample Planning Calendar (K–1) for Stations Roll-Out and Refresh

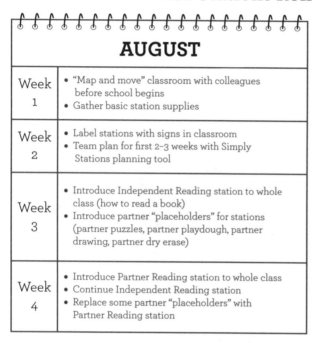

AUGUST

Week 1	• "Map and move" classroom with colleagues before school begins • Gather basic station supplies
Week 2	• Label stations with signs in classroom • Team plan for first 2–3 weeks with Simply Stations planning tool
Week 3	• Introduce Independent Reading station to whole class (how to read a book) • Introduce partner "placeholders" for stations (partner puzzles, partner playdough, partner drawing, partner dry erase)
Week 4	• Introduce Partner Reading station to whole class • Continue Independent Reading station • Replace some partner "placeholders" with Partner Reading station

SEPTEMBER

Week 1	• Introduce Listening and Speaking station • Use checklist for operating listening before sending kids there • Introduce Word Study station using kids' names • Replace some partner "placeholders"
Week 2	• Introduce Poetry station with familiar nursery rhymes and poems • Replace some partner "placeholders" • Introduce the management board
Week 3	• Introduce Writing station with lists and bucket fillers • Introduce Let's Talk station with describing photos • Replace some partner "placeholders" • Refresh Independent Reading and Partner Reading stations
Week 4	• Introduce Drama station • Refresh Listening and Speaking and Word Study stations

OCTOBER

Week 1	• Refresh Poetry and Writing stations • Introduce Inquiry and Research station
Week 2	• Refresh Let's Talk and Drama stations
Week 3	• Refresh Independent Reading and Partner Reading stations
Week 4	• Refresh Listening and Speaking and Word Study stations

NOVEMBER

Week 1	• Refresh Poetry and Writing stations
Week 2	• Refresh Let's Talk and Drama stations
Week 3	
Week 4	• Refresh Inquiry and Research station

DECEMBER

Week 1	• Refresh Independent Reading and Partner Reading stations
Week 2	• Refresh Listening and Speaking and Word Study stations
Week 3	
Week 4	

JANUARY

Week 1	• Refresh Poetry and Writing stations
Week 2	• Refresh Let's Talk and Drama stations
Week 3	• Refresh Inquiry and Research station
Week 4	• Refresh Independent Reading and Partner Reading stations

FEBRUARY

Week 1	• Refresh Listening and Speaking and Word Study stations
Week 2	• Refresh Poetry and Writing stations
Week 3	• Refresh Let's Talk and Drama stations
Week 4	• Refresh Inquiry and Research station

MARCH

Week 1	• Refresh Independent Reading and Partner Reading stations
Week 2	• Refresh Listening and Speaking and Word Study stations
Week 3	• Refresh Poetry and Writing stations
Week 4	• Refresh Let's Talk and Drama stations

APRIL

Week 1	• Refresh Inquiry and Research station
Week 2	• Refresh Independent Reading and Partner Reading stations
Week 3	• Refresh Listening and Speaking and Word Study stations
Week 4	• Refresh Poetry and Writing stations

MAY

Week 1	• Refresh Let's Talk and Drama stations
Week 2	• Refresh Inquiry and Research station
Week 3	• Refresh stations as needed
Week 4	• Refresh stations as needed • Reflect and make notes for next year

NOTES

Rotate the table group placeholder activities for the first week or two of school while you begin teaching things that can move into literacy stations. For example, as you read books aloud, place them in a basket in the classroom library to start the Independent Reading station. During read-aloud, teach kindergartners to think and talk about characters. When you introduce the Listening and Speaking station, students will be ready to listen for characters and talk about them. As you begin Writing Workshop, model how to draw pictures and add labels about people and things kids know. Include names of children in your class. When you introduce the Writing station, children can practice writing their names and those of their classmates. They can draw and label pictures, too.

Starting the second or third week of school, replace placeholders with literacy stations, one at a time, until you've eventually phased out table group activities. Within the first month or so, you should have several literacy stations up and running. Small group instruction should start between the sixth and eighth week of kindergarten.

Literacy Stations Management Board How-To

After you've established several literacy stations in your classroom, you can help children work independently by setting up a management board. The management board will save time by showing kids where to go throughout stations time without you having to direct them every step of the way. Once children know how to read the management board and understand what to do at stations, you can simply dismiss them (several at a time) to their first station.

Setting Up the Management Board

Feel free to adjust any of the following ideas to create a system that works for you and your students. For instance, many teachers I've worked with over the years prefer a simple management board made with a pocket chart. Another idea is to put magnetic tape on the back of cards and place them on a magnetic whiteboard. Or, you can project a management board on a screen using a PowerPoint template. You can even embed a digital timer in it! No matter how you present the management board, the basic structure will remain the same. In the end, the goal is for students to be able to refer to it independently during stations time.

Photo by Matthew Rood.

The directions that follow are for creating a traditional management board with a pocket chart in a self-contained classroom.

iStock.com

① Start by taking a photo of each of your students and/or write their names on individual cards that fit in a pocket chart. A 3-x-5 size name card usually works well.

② Make icon cards to match each station you'll have. You'll find icon printables at **resources.corwin.com/simplystations-writing**, or you can take photos of each station to use as an icon instead. You'll need two copies of each icon, one for the first rotation, and another for the second rotation. (If you decide to have three rotations, make three copies of each icon.) And, if you duplicate stations, you may want to number the extras (e.g., Writing station 1, Writing station 2, and so on). I've included a Letter Writing icon to use if you want to vary what students do at the Writing station over time.

③ Pair students using photos/name cards on the left side of the pocket chart. (This is important, because we want kids to read from left to right.) If you have an odd number of students, you could have one group of three, or a child could work alone.

In a first-grade classroom, the teacher uses photos of the students and their accompanying station icons on a pocket chart. She uses Meet With Teacher cards to show which students she will meet with during small group instruction today while the rest of the class is at literacy stations.

④ To keep children from losing their partners during small group, consider pairing children who are in the same flexible reading group. You'll find that students working on the same level push each other forward.

⑤ Place two icon cards beside each pair of students to show which stations they'll go to each day. (These show where students go for the first rotation, then the second rotation.) If you have students go to three rotations, place three icon cards beside each pair of students.

⑥ Print Meet With Teacher cards for each pair of students you meet with in small group for that rotation. (For example, if you're meeting with four students in small group, you'll need two Meet With Teacher cards.) Place the Meet With Teacher cards over an icon card in the first or second rotation, depending when you'll meet a group.

Now the management board is ready for kids to read when they enter your room. Teach them to read it on their own so they can quickly and easily go to stations during literacy stations time.

Daily Use of the Management Board

a. At the start of stations/small group time, dismiss several students at a time to go to their first station. Having only a few kids moving at once simplifies classroom management and prevents a chaotic start to stations time. You want children to move calmly and quietly to their station and get started right away. Playing calm background music during stations time may help.

b. Use an audible signal (bell, chime, music) when it's time to switch to the next rotation. This may take some practice, but kids usually get the hang of it within a few days. Some teachers use an online timer with a built-in message that it's time to switch.

c. At the end of each day, simply remove your Meet With Teacher cards and place them to the side. Rotate literacy stations icons down to the next space on the board. Then place tomorrow's Meet With Teacher cards over the top of stations icons beside the children you'll meet with next in the first or second small group rotation.

d. Finally, look over the board to be sure children will be practicing at stations where they'll get the most benefit. You may decide to move a station icon to match what a particular pair of students needs most. For example, if you notice that two students are scheduled to go to the Partner Reading station but they really need more time to write, move the Writing station icon beside their names and move the Partner Reading icon to another spot for children who need more opportunities to practice reading with a partner.

You might use a PowerPoint for your management board projected for the class to see during stations. Integrate a timer if you'd like, too.

This upper-grade teacher used a small space on a dry-erase magnetic whiteboard for her management board. She used photos of each station as icons and wrote the names of stations and who would go there under the station.

Jada	Miguel	Partner Reading Station	Writing Station	Logan	Makayla
Ava	Xavier	Meet With Teacher	Poetry Station	Noah	Alyssa
Gabriella	Jordan	Meet With Teacher	Drama Station	Maverick	Destiny
Amelia	Jayden	Independent Reading Station	Partner Reading Station	Josh	Emma
Genevieve	Gabriel	Independent Reading Station	Listening and Speaking Station	Zach	Martina

Portion of the management board in a departmentalized upper-grade classroom.

Class 1 is pictured on the left with green cards.

Class 2 is on the right with pink cards. Move the icons (not the names) down a space daily.

Meet With Teacher icons are inserted daily.

2 Writing Station Basics

Why Include This Station?

Writing independently builds confident writers who choose to write on their own.

Practice at a Writing station combined with a daily independent writing time for the whole class as part of your daily literacy block is important because writing on their own

- Gives students ownership as *they* choose what to write and become members of a writing community

- Helps kids apply what they're learning about being a writer

- Improves children's composition, vocabulary, and writing fluency skills, especially as they set writing goals and work toward these

- Allows students to strengthen reading-writing connections and relate to authors

Just as students become better readers by reading, they become better writers by writing! Giving them blank journals and pencils is a start, but it isn't enough to ensure that all students will succeed as writers. Children become more skilled as writers by having opportunities to participate in a structured writing time every day at school—time where the teacher models how to get ideas, put them on paper, and craft them followed by independent writing time for kids. In my experience, Writing Workshop is a good starting point for the Writing station. But a Writing station can be implemented to enhance any writing curriculum.

Writing is hard work. Children need to be encouraged and nurtured to think; generate their own ideas; record them by speaking, drawing, and writing; and share them with others. Effective writing instruction requires several key components:

- Teacher modeling: Set aside time daily that includes a few minutes to model writing in front of your class or show students models of writing in picture books.

- Independent writing time with clear expectations: Students need at least ten to twenty minutes of time every day to practice writing on their own. Provide supports to help kids write—and want to write.

EL TIP: Use wordless books with multilingual students and encourage children to tell stories about the pictures. Help them add labels to pictures as a first step in writing in a new language.

- Conferring time: Meet with children one on one to set and check on specific writing goals. A printable Conferring About Writing Goals template can be found at **resources.corwin.com/simplystations-writing** for you to use during independent writing time.

- Sharing time: Allow five to eight minutes for students to share what they've written with each other in small groups or with the entire class.

The Writing station is typically introduced in primary grades after a few weeks of school. You'll want to have plenty of time to establish the writing instructional routines outlined above to give students tools they can use for practice at the Writing station. In upper grades, you can open a Writing station as soon as you've had a chance to model your expectations for what kids will do here. See the Launch Lessons on page 40 for ideas.

The teacher writes and thinks aloud in front of her class before they transition to independent writing time.

The main thing children do at this station is work as writers. This, of course, involves reading and thinking, too! The writing children do may look very different from one developmental stage to the next and from one grade level to another. (In Section 4 and on the companion website I've included an Early Developmental Writing Stages chart with writing samples to help you think about what pre-emergent and emergent writers might do.)

At the Writing station, your students will be generating ideas, composing texts, revising their writing, and publishing things for others to read. Help children set a purpose and make a plan for writing to increase the benefits at this station; you'll see more about this idea in Section 3 when we lean in to teaching for transfer. Teach students about author's craft and conventions in whole group writing, and hold students accountable for using these skills at the Writing station, too. Help children set individual writing goals and remind them to work toward their goals as they write on their own or with a partner. Remember, the Writing station connects to concepts and genres you've taught with in whole group based on your curriculum, standards, and students' needs. (Again, Section 3 of this book digs deeper into planning for, teaching, and rolling out stations with clear intent.)

Students work at a Writing station using what they've learned over time from Writing Workshop.

EL TIP: Before writing, have multilingual learners talk about what they will write, and sketch and jot down ideas as rehearsal. They might record themselves and listen back before trying to write the words.

Writing goals posted at the Writing station.

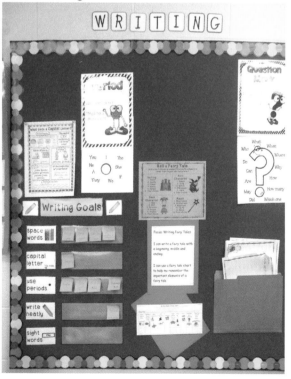

When considering materials to include at the Writing station, think about what and why you want students to write on their own as well as the needs of the children who are working there. Be sure to provide supports that match their developmental needs so they can work independently of you. (A list of materials for different writing stages is provided in Section 4.) Also consider the interests of your students when adding supplies to the Writing station. Periodically including new supplies can motivate kids to write and make it more fun. Let them make stuff, like books or cards, too, along with writing in the genres outlined in your standards. Having an audience can also increase writing motivation. Provide authentic materials (blank cards, notebook paper, and colorful stickers instead of forms to fill in) and authentic writing experiences, like book reviews to post in the classroom library, letters that are mailed to real people, and stories or poems that are published online for others to read.

Kids make cards at the Writing station using supports provided.

What Do Students Do
at This Station?

Children write on their own and practice writing strategies for craft and conventions modeled during whole group instruction.

This is what you should see at the Writing station:

- A pair of children write on their own or together.

- Two or three students sit comfortably at a small table, by a countertop, or at two desks near a writing display area (bulletin board, wall space, or display board).

- Writing anchor charts made with the class related to craft and conventions are posted here for students to refer to while writing.

- Several kinds of paper (plain unlined, handwriting, or notebook paper), and a few writing implements (sharpened pencils, pens, or markers) are organized and easy for kids to access.

- Class-made samples of writing genres they have explored together are posted here with labels (e.g., *I can write . . . a story, a letter, an information brochure, my opinion*).

- Students are writing with tools that match their developmental level (e.g., blank paper and pencils early in kindergarten; notebook paper and pens in upper grades).

- Children use writing resources (e.g., alphabet strip with pictures in K–1 or a thesaurus in Grades 2–4) that have been taught with during whole group writing instruction.

- This station can be duplicated, so several pairs of children may be writing fiction at one Writing station and writing nonfiction at another. (A variety of other stations are in use during this time, too! See other books in the Simply Stations series for ideas.)

- Students may talk with their partner, discuss ideas they want to write about, tell stories, or ask questions about each other's work.

- Children may be writing summaries or book reviews to be posted in the classroom library/Independent Reading station.

A pair of kindergartners work at a table at a Writing station.

Two desks create a Writing station near a bulletin board for displaying writing samples.

Two fourth graders work at a countertop converted to a Writing station.

Here is a sampling of the types of work students may do at a Writing station with a partner or on their own. (Ideas on how to develop these are found in Section 3 of this book.) Pairs of students may be

- Choosing what to write about by talking, thinking, sketching, or browsing model texts

- Talking about what they'll write with a partner, such as

  - A story idea

  - A book they want to write and illustrate

  - A get-well card for an absent classmate

- Continuing to work on a piece of writing from independent writing time

- Making a plan for their writing by drawing, jotting, or using a simple graphic organizer

- Crafting a piece of writing alone or together (e.g., a narrative, an informational text, an opinion piece)

- Writing responses to books read

- Adding details to or choosing more descriptive words for their writing

- Peer editing each other's writing

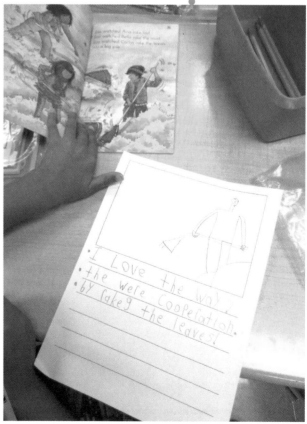

Students write responses at the Writing station.

To utilize a Writing station effectively in your classroom, brainstorm with your students what they might do here. I like to create an I Can list, such as the pictured samples that follow, to clarify expectations for this station. The I Can list helps students work independently in the station, and it helps clarify learning expectations; they'll start to see the connections between your instruction and what they do in stations.

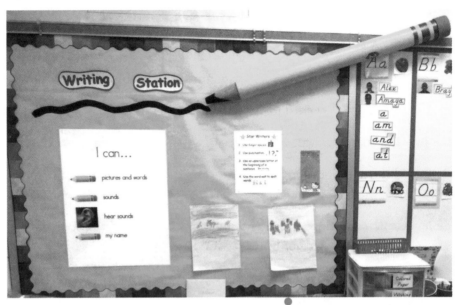

These pictorial I Can lists were made with primary students and posted at the Writing station.

An intermediate I Can list reflects what older students do at a Writing station.

We can:

- work on a personal narrative
- revise a piece from our portfolio
- write a response to a book we read
- peer edit
- revisit a model text for ideas

How Do I Keep This Station Varied *and* Fresh?

To keep the Writing station fresh and running smoothly throughout the year, try these suggestions:

- "Refresh" your Writing station about every three weeks by changing out some of the materials or what kids might write there. Use the planning calendars in Section 4 (printables available online) to schedule this ahead of time. Consider what you've been teaching students to do as writers as you add new things for them to practice.

- Include a space to display several children's writing on a revolving basis. Change this display every week or two, so everyone has a chance to be in the spotlight.

- Add authentic paper (instead of run-off worksheets) periodically. You might try colored paper, stationery from a discount store, white paper stapled into little books, fronts of old greeting cards that can be reused, envelopes, skinny list paper, or lined index cards for postcards. Limit the number of pieces students may use at one time to keep them from disappearing too quickly! Also, when you add something, remove something else to keep the choices from becoming overwhelming.

- Change out writing utensils every few weeks. Start with a few sharpened pencils. Then add a few thin markers or colored pencils. Or use ballpoint pens (just be sure to model how to edit with these by crossing out words). Don't put out too many materials or too much at once! Make your expectations clear—this is a Writing station (so it doesn't turn into a place where kids draw and never get to writing).

- This is a fun place to include a few seasonal materials. Easy does it, though. (See the Seasonal Writing Ideas list in Section 4.)

- You might convert the Writing station into a News station for a fun twist. If you do Daily News or Morning Message as part of your daily routine in Grades K–2, you might include a Daily News or Morning Message station. (See Section 4 for more ideas.)

- Add and change out word banks for children to use at the Writing station to encourage them to use new vocabulary. Make these *with* your class and model how to use them as you write in front of your class to get the most from them. (A few samples are included in Section 4, and you can download printables online.)

- Add new kinds of writing for students to practice on your *"I can write…"* labels and samples on the display space of your Writing station. For example, young children may start the year by writing their names and labels; but later in the year they will be writing nonfiction books and stories.

- Include correspondence writing at this station as you teach children how to write letters. You might include special paper; there is printable stationery available on the companion website (**resources.corwin .com/simplystations-writing**). Children may also enjoy making cards from paper folded in half with envelopes or postcards from blank index cards. Provide samples to use as models.

- Add photos of things that relate to your students to spur ideas for writing. For example, post pictures of kids in the cafeteria, students playing at recess, events from your school carnival, or a field trip your class took.

- Periodically post a fine art print to use as writing inspiration. Model how to write about what a picture makes you think of or feel before asking your kids to do the same.

- Use "bucket fillers" as small bits for kids to write. They simply write encouraging notes to classmates. Model this, too.

- Add props occasionally to make writing fun. I like to use little stuffed animals, small plastic objects, or natural objects. Again, model your own writing with these before asking students to work independently here.

- Model with and then place stickers, stamps, or emojis at this station to add interest. Limit how many kids may use so they don't spend the whole time playing with the new materials instead of writing!

- Place "author study" materials nearby. Use books and information from whole group instruction that kids can refer to after you've modeled with these.

- Teach children how to use a stapler or Scotch tape to add on to their pieces. Same for a date stamp to show how many days they've been working on a piece of writing. (They simply stamp their writing with today's date.)

- Include digital options for writing. (See Section 4 for specific ideas.)

Write about things our class has done.

ride the bus

picked pumpkins

Photos related to familiar topics posted at the Writing station gives kids ideas of things they might write about.

playground fun

blowing bubbles

Kids write bucket fillers for classmates at the Writing station.

First grader uses two stickers to compose a story at the Writing station.

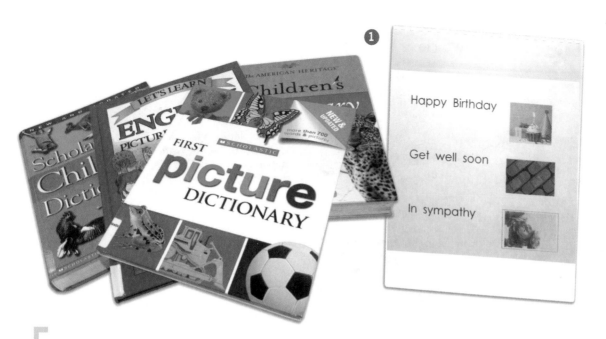

What Are *the* Essential Materials?

Whether the Writing station is stationary or portable, there are several basic materials you'll want to include. Design it to help children easily access resources that will help them do their best writing. Use what you have at your school to get started. Here are some materials you'll want as you set up a Writing station.

1. Picture dictionaries, class-made word banks, or thesaurus to help with word choice

2. Two or three comfortable seats

3. Small table or two desks placed near a wall or display space

4. Tiny lights, paper globes, a large pencil or something fun to create interest in this space

5. A few pencils or pens that encourage writing

6. Bulletin board to display class-made writing samples and anchor charts

7. Paper organized for easy access

8. Class-made samples to match writing genre labels

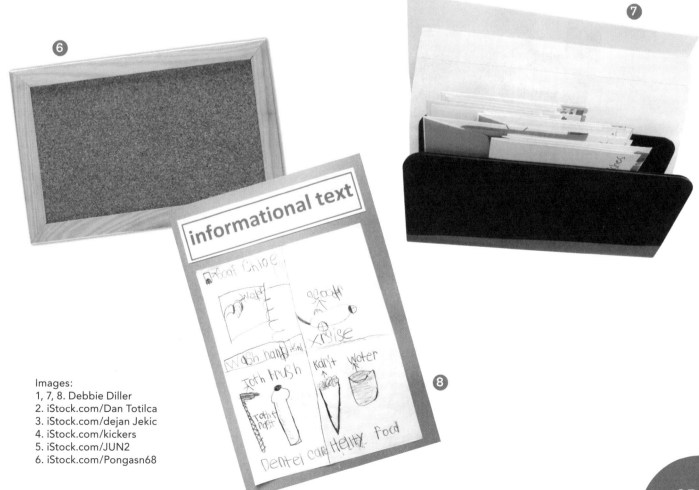

informational text

Images:
1, 7, 8. Debbie Diller
2. iStock.com/Dan Totilca
3. iStock.com/dejan Jekic
4. iStock.com/kickers
5. iStock.com/JUN2
6. iStock.com/Pongasn68

How Do I Set Up This Station?

Place a small table or two desks with a couple of kid-sized seats near a board or display space to create a stationary Writing station, if possible. Try to choose a spot near the word wall, so students can easily access words you want them to spell correctly. Post writing anchor charts and models of writing here as you teach with them. Hang them at children's eye level to make it easy for them to use these resources.

Setting up the "bones" of the Writing station before school starts. A small table is placed near boards covered in black paper. The word wall will go on the right, and the board on the left will be used for displaying writing samples and supports.

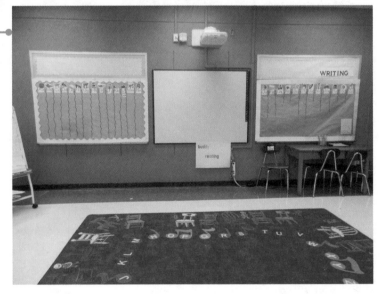

The word wall is on boards beside an interactive whiteboard and provides the backdrop for the Writing station (on the right) in first grade.

Include writing tools, such as paper and pencils. Organize writing tools so children can easily use them. I like to use labeled stacking trays for paper and a small container for pens or pencils. Don't put out too many materials at once. This will help kids get to work writing (rather than spending most of their time searching for what they want to use). Provide help for choosing what to write about at the Writing station. This is an age-old problem: What should I write about today? You might post a heart map, a few photos for inspiration, and a word bank or two with photos for help. Model how to get ideas for writing before expecting students to do this on their own at the Writing station. See Timeless Standard 1 for more ideas.

Above all, make your Writing station inviting—a place where kids *want* to write! It should be an easy to see, standout space that communicates that writing is important in your classroom. And remember that you can duplicate this station if you'd like. You might use a countertop space by a window (that doubles as "wall space") if you have one. You could have a Fiction Writing and a separate Nonfiction Writing station. Or you might number the icons and matching signs Writing 1 or Writing 2 so kids know where to work.

If you decide to have a portable Writing station, use a container that holds the supplies children will need. Place paper in labeled folders and pencils in a zipper bag. Have students use these materials near the word wall. You might add a trifold board with mini writing anchor charts and writing samples for them to use, too.

EL TIP: Word cards with matching photos will provide support and give multilingual students ideas of things to write about. Be sure to model well with these cards before expecting kids to do this independently.

TIME-SAVING TIP: Ask students to find interesting photos in magazines or online that could be placed in the Writing station to generate ideas. Staple these to a display board. Or, place the pictures in clear plastic sleeves to be used year after year. Only display a few at a time to preserve the novelty!

This upper-grade Writing station is made from several desks against a wall. Labeled containers hold finished and unfinished work.

A third-grade station occupies a small space by a bulletin board to display student writing samples and supports.

How Do I Introduce *the* Writing Station?

Model expectations; reteach as necessary.

It's vital that you model what you expect at a station so that children know exactly what to do and how to do it. Model, model, model! And don't be afraid to stop and reteach if students aren't using materials correctly. Remember that one of the best things you can do is to engage your class in whole group writing time every day. Include modeled writing, independent writing and conferring time, and sharing so your students learn how to write. The Writing station is simply an extension of that time. Here are some step-by-step procedures to help you introduce the Writing station. (Also see the Launch Lesson on page 40 for introducing this station.)

1. Remind children that anything they're learning to do as writers is what they will practice at the Writing station. They may even continue to work on a piece from independent writing time at this station. (You might keep their writing folders near the Writing station and show them how to pull out a piece they're working on.)

2. To help students get the most from their time at the Writing station, show them how to choose what to write about using materials in this space. Be sure you've modeled with these well before asking students to do this on their own! Model how to think about the following:

    a. What will you write? (topic)

    b. Who is your audience? (reader)

    c. Why are you writing this? (author's purpose)

    Also see Timeless Standard 1 lessons in Section 3 for how to generate writing ideas.

3. Demonstrate how to think about and use writing materials at this station and how to put them away neatly so others can easily find what they need. Model the following:

a. What kind of paper will I use? (list paper, a card and envelope, speech bubble pages, something from my independent writing folder)

b. What will I write with? (pencil, pen, marker)

c. What models will I use? (a picture book, a word list, an ABC chart)

4. Model and remind children to use these three steps when writing. A copy of this graphic is included in the online companion at **resources.corwin.com/simplystations-writing** so you can display it at the Writing station.

Images: iStock.com; shutterstock.com

5. Make your expectations clear, including things such as

a. You must write something.

b. Please make ONE thing—a list or a card or a story.

c. Think about your reader. Make it neat!

6. Model how to put materials away carefully so they are ready for the next children using this station. If you have a portable Writing station, show how to lay materials out carefully when starting and then put them back into the container neatly when finished.

7. In whole group lessons using modeled and shared writing, think aloud about everything you do as a writer. Over time, move these same metacognitive skills into the Writing station for students to practice when writing alone or working with a partner. See Section 3 for ideas.

TIME-SAVING TIP: Post a photo of what the Writing station should look like when you're done there to save time at cleanup.

LAUNCH LESSONS for the WRITING STATION

Here are sample lessons to use for the Writing station. Routines for independent writing will be taught during whole group writing instruction as well. Plan for an independent writing time for the whole class daily and include the opportunity for pairs of students to go to the Writing station for additional writing time during stations each day.

You can break this lesson into several parts, depending on the age and experience of students in your classroom.

INTRODUCING HOW TO WRITE INDEPENDENTLY

- First, demonstrate how to choose independently what to write about and ask students to do the same. Start with something simple that *all* children in your class can be successful with. See the list in Section 4 of possible kinds of writing to do with grade-level suggestions for ideas.

  ○ Say: *Choose to write about something you know and care about. I'm going to write a bucket filler for someone in our class. Daniella has been ill, so I'm writing a note to put in her cubby to welcome her back when she returns.*

  Over the next few weeks, continue to model how to get writing ideas. View videos by authors where they tell about their idea sources. Make a list with your students of where to get ideas. See Timeless Standard 1 for suggested lessons.

- Read aloud books you know your students will love during whole group reading instruction, and then over time return to these books during whole group writing instruction to study what writers do. Choose books that support reading-writing connections. Pay special attention to the personal interests of your students, especially those who don't seem particularly interested in writing. Also teach students how to think about the tools they'll need for the kind of writing they'll do.

  ○ Say: *I'm writing a short bucket filler, so I'll need a small piece of paper. Word wall words and spelling pattern charts will help me with spelling. I'll write neatly so Daniella can easily read what I wrote. The handwriting chart can help me form letters I'm still having trouble with.*

  ○ Or say: *I will write an information book, so I'm stapling together several pieces of blank white paper. My topic will be rocks, because I know a lot about them. I'm going to use the read aloud book on rocks from last week for ideas, and then I'll look online for photos of rocks to use, too.*

- Remind your class to always think, then write, then read as they compose!

- Make your expectations for writing clear. Create a chart with your students, using their words, to post at the Writing station. Write picture directions with your class, if needed, on the chart for easy reference. See samples in the photos on this spread.

  ○ Say: *When you go to the Writing station, you can write by your-self or with your partner. Before you write, read the expectations as a reminder of what to do here. If you need help, talk with your partner. I'll be working with a small group and won't be able to help you during this time. But I can help you during independent writing time if you need help then.*

- During independent writing time, give students ample time to write on their own. Walk around the class and have brief conferences with individuals about what they're writing. Take anecdotal notes to help you remember and learn about your kids as writers. Help children establish writing goals and check in with their progress as they're working.

- Over time, introduce peer editing to your class. See Timeless Standard 5 for ideas on how to teach this and then move it to the Writing station for additional practice.

- Introduce the Writing station as soon as students show they understand what to do as a writer. Remind children they can work on a piece from independent writing time at the Writing station if they'd like. Or, they can write something new.

The teacher confers with individuals during independent writing time to get to know them as writers.

TIME-SAVING TIP:
The more you model and confer during independent writing time and let kids write, the better your students will do at the Writing station. Simply move what you've taught kids to do as writers to the Writing station over time.

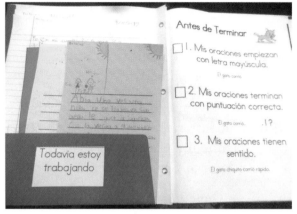

Each student has a portfolio to store writing during Writing Workshop. They can access this at the Writing station, too.

INTRODUCING RESPONSE TO YOUR PARTNER'S WRITING

- After students have had time to write, model how to take a few minutes to respond to your partner's writing. Do this in whole class writing instruction first before moving this task to the Writing station. Have two partners model this for the class.

  ○ Say: *After you write, take a few minutes to respond to each other's writing. One partner can be the reader and the other the listener. The reader reads a bit of the writing he did. The listener tells what she heard and may ask questions. Then switch parts and read the other partner's writing.*

  ○ Or: *After writing, you can do peer editing. Remember that the writer listens to your partner read your piece to you. Only the writer can write things on his paper. Don't write on each other's papers.*

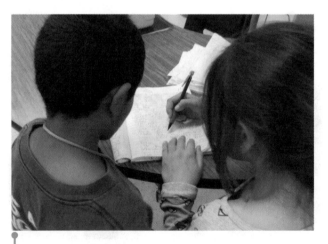

Fourth-graders work together to peer edit.

INTRODUCING THE SPACE

- Gather students near your Writing station. Children may have to cluster around a small table you've set up, but be sure they can all see the materials there. Explain that this will be the special spot where they work on writing during stations time.

- Show them the available tools at this station—from the kinds of writing they might do (posted on the display board) to sharpened pencils and a variety of paper in containers. If you've included model texts or a thesaurus, remind students how and why they'd use these. Tell kids you'll be adding different kinds of writing to this station as they learn new things to do as writers. Ask students for their ideas on anything else they might need at the Writing station.

- Set the purpose for this station, and model how to use the materials here. (You might have several pairs of students take turns modeling what this will look like, too.)

  - Say: *At the Writing station, you and your partner will choose what to write about first. It's okay to talk with your partner about what you're writing. But most of the time you should be writing at this station.*

  - Continue: *Use the tools at the Writing station to help you. Look at the word wall to spell those words. Use charts for other words you might want to spell. Think about your writing goals as you work. Think about who will read what you wrote, too. Be sure your writing is clear and easy to read.*

INTRODUCING CLEANUP

- Model how to return materials carefully and quietly when it is time to clean up. Show how to return writing materials to the appropriate places.

  - Say: *When you're finished writing, return materials neatly where they belong so others can use them. If you used crayons or pencils, place them in the labeled cups. If you have extra paper you didn't use, put it back with the paper it matches. If you worked on a piece from Writing Workshop, place it in your writing folder. Pieces you are still working on should go in the Things I'm Working On section. When I give the cleanup signal, put things away quietly and carefully. Put the materials back neatly, like this. That will make it easy for whoever uses the Writing station to find what they need.*

EL TIP: Be sure to ask multilingual students to model how to use the Writing station, too. These opportunities to use oral language will build skill and confidence.

TRYING IT OUT

- Have your class practice independent writing at their seats before opening the Writing station. After you've introduced this station, you might have pairs of students practice writing here during independent writing time to demonstrate that they understand expectations. Wait to open this station until classroom writing routines are well-established so students understand your expectations of them as writers.

- Once kids know how to write on their own, you might seat them in pairs and have them talk with each other before and after they write.

All students write during independent writing time.

KEEPING IT GOING

- In whole group writing lessons, continue to model how to generate ideas for writing, how to organize your ideas, and how to add details to your writing. Expose students to writing in various forms, such as lists, personal narratives, letters, informational text, postcards, thank you notes, and opinions. (Consult your state standards for specifics.)

- Provide time daily for students to share their writing with each other.

- Over time, move these same strategies and genres into the Writing station for students to practice when working alone or with a partner. (See Section 3 for lesson ideas.)

- Continue having an independent writing time daily as part of your literacy block throughout the school year for the whole class. And provide additional writing practice at the Writing station, too.

What Are Some Signs *of* Success?

You'll want students to be accountable for using time and resources wisely during independent writing time and at the Writing station. Children may share with the class what they did or learned at this station during a five- to ten-minute class Reflection Time following stations/small group time. I like to begin by asking whoever was at the Writing station to share what they wrote today with the class. They may also send a photo or recording to their teacher and/or family via an app like Remind, Seesaw, or ClassDojo. They may tell about a writing strategy they used at this station. Or, they might note what they tried related to their writing goals. A printable Conferring About Writing Goals template can be found on the online companion at **resources .corwin.com/simplystations-writing**.

TIME-SAVING TIP: Pay attention to students' comments during Reflection Time, as they're great indicators of when to refresh or modify a station.

Other indicators you'll notice when observing for a successful Writing station include the following:

- Students are engaged in thinking and writing most of the time. They are seated and are focused on what they are writing.

- Kids choose to write something they *know about*, *care about*, and *can* write without adult assistance. They know how to get ideas for writing on their own.

- Partners may be brainstorming ideas, jotting down notes, making a list, or organizing their writing. They keep working even when they get stuck.

- Students spend most of their time writing in whatever fashion they can, for example, drawing a picture and labeling it, sound out spelling words as best they can, using a yellow crayon to circle words they're unsure of, crossing out words they want to delete, or adding details to pictures.

- Children use writing resources found at the Writing station. They use the word wall, picture dictionaries, word lists with matching photos, class-made samples, and other things the teacher has modeled with previously.

- Before writing, students talk with each other about what they will write, why they are writing this, and who their audience is.

- After writing, partners share what they wrote and give feedback to each other.

- Children can tell you what they're doing at this station and the strategies they're using. For example, *I'm writing a story with my partner. I'm working on my writing goal: I am adding details to help my reader visualize. We like sharing our writing with each other because we get ideas of new things to write. I use my finger to make spaces between words, like this. That helps the reader understand what I wrote.*

- Students care for materials and put them back when finished so others can easily find and use them.

Once students show that they are practicing with automaticity, it's time to change things up. For example, if Grades K–1 students can easily generate all kinds of lists and spell with greater ease and you've taught them how to make simple books, it may be time to change up what they are practicing at the Writing station. Simply change out list writing paper and list samples for blank paper stapled into little books along with samples of class-made books. Generate ideas of what they might want to make books about and post at the Writing station.

If older students are tiring of personal narratives, switch to another genre, such as writing poems. Be sure you've modeled this type of writing well before asking kids to do this without your help. And provide model texts at the station for reference, too.

If you notice that students aren't doing what you expect at the Writing station, don't allow off-task behavior to persist. Have them sit near your small group teaching table to think about their behavior before allowing them to return to that station. Be specific in calling attention to preferred behaviors, especially during Reflection Time. Reteach as needed. Use Launch Lessons throughout the year as reminders, too.

Also try to figure out *why* students are off-task. Perhaps you need to provide more writing support at this station. Or maybe you've asked certain children to do something they're not yet ready to do on their own. Be sure to provide familiar materials and tasks students *can* do as writers.

Troubleshooting Tips

IF YOU NOTICE THIS	TRY THIS
Children don't write much at the Writing station.	Model, model, model! Unless you've modeled *how* to write well during Writing Workshop, some kids won't know what to do as writers and may just sit there. Students will write more when they experience *success* as writers. Include things they *can* do here, such as list-writing or writing poems (after you've modeled how to write these forms).
Students just copy samples at the Writing station.	Again, be sure you've modeled *how* to write well. Provide resources, such as word lists with matching photos you've modeled with, so kids can use these as they write.
Young kids are scribbling rather than writing at the Writing station.	Look at these children's development as writers. Are they still at the scribble stage? Or are they making mock letters? See the Early Developmental Writing Stages chart in Section 4 (printable available at the companion website) for ideas.
Children are coloring rather than writing.	Closely examine materials you've provided. If you give kids pictures to be colored, that's what many will choose to do. Provide writing paper instead of cute forms to fill in.
Students waste time because they can't figure out what to write independently.	As a class, review how writers get ideas, and post these at the Writing station. Use heart maps, writer's notebooks, or photos of things your class has studied or done.
Children don't put materials away neatly.	Put labels on stacking trays for kinds of paper, cups for pencils or crayons, and a crate for writing portfolios. Don't put out too many materials at once—just a few pencils or markers. Post a photo of what the Writing station should look like when it's cleaned up.
Students use up materials quickly. They use a bunch of your pre-stapled books or stickers without writing much.	Don't put out too many things at once. Set parameters for use of special materials. Tell children they may make *one* of something—one list or one book. Or, they may use five stickers, three stamps, etc.
Writing is sloppy and poorly done.	When students have an audience (other than the teacher) for their writing and a purpose (other than the teacher said to write this), their writing will improve. Have whoever was at the Writing station today share a bit of their writing with the class during Reflection Time daily.

Planning and Teaching

Now that you have the routines in place for a Writing Station, let's look at how to teach students to work authentically with purpose there. It's important to remember, as you're planning literacy instruction and practice with stations, that the ultimate goal is transfer. Literacy stations are not just time-filler activities to keep kids busy while you're meeting with small groups. Station work should be directly connected to your whole group instruction over time, which is directly connected to standards. It all ties together intentionally, by design and through your expertise as a teacher.

As students have opportunities to practice what you've modeled well in writing, they will learn to communicate more effectively—generating and organizing their ideas, choosing words thoughtfully, and considering purpose and audience. It takes a lot of practice to get proficient at something, and just giving kids a chance to practice on the day you've taught something isn't enough for most of them. If you want to improve practice at literacy stations, it begins with solid instruction and established routines for ongoing practice.

With that in mind, in this section of the book you'll find ideas for how to plan and teach strong lessons that students will eventually practice over and over again across a school year with another student at the Writing station. Each piece begins with explicit instruction centered on a timeless literacy standard related to writing.

Instead of using standards from each state, I'm using what I refer to as *timeless literacy standards*. These standards may vary slightly in wording from state to state, but they all are pieces that will remain no matter where you're teaching or what the current education movement is. Please change the language slightly, as needed, to match the standards in your school system.

In this section, I've broken down five timeless literacy standards, one at a time, to focus on crucial literacy skills related to writing. You'll find suggestions for how to teach and model each skill well during whole group, and then move it to the Writing station where students will practice together with a classmate. Students will practice multiple times throughout the year to provide spiral review—recurring practice that helps students transfer learning. It begins with teaching students to write with intention during modeled writing and independent writing. You'll be modeling and thinking aloud to show kids what they will eventually be doing in pairs at the Writing station.

When students show that they understand **what** to do, **how** to do it, and can tell **why**, it's time to move that work into the Writing station. Be intentional, and the children you teach will be, too. For example, it's time to move the work from Timeless Writing Standard 2 (*The student will write and revise stories with characters, sequenced events, and descriptive details.*) into the Writing station when students can do the following in whole group writing time:

- Generate ideas for stories

- Create characters that interact with each other in their stories

- Write a story that includes sequenced events with a beginning, middle, and end

- Add descriptive details to their stories as they revise

- Use time order words as they write events in order

The more students work with these concepts over time, the deeper their learning will go, and the more apt they will be to apply what you've been modeling.

Start *With* Solid Planning

Good instruction (and subsequent practice) begins with planning. I've seen the best results when teachers work together as a grade-level team to plan literacy instruction and connected practice at stations. Yes, it may seem time consuming, but you'll get more fluent the more you work together. Come to your team planning meetings prepared. Look at your curriculum documents to get an idea of which writing standards are coming up in the next few weeks. Have formative and summative assessment data in hand to think about students' needs, too. Examine student writing samples as a team. Then plan together for big ideas based on your school, district, and state learning standards—and keeping your students' needs in mind—using suggestions from this section of this book. I've included tips for choosing model texts for writing that you can reuse when you teach reading. Think about what you've tried in the past and share successes and things that didn't go so well (and why).

You might use a big piece of chart paper and markers to plan together. Or have someone type and project your planning chart onto a screen you can all see and access. Or work in a Google Doc or on your school's platform. Your choice!

The Simply Stations Planning Tool (see the printable online) is purposely simple and customizable, but it's the best way I've found to teach with intention from standards through whole group and into stations. Of course, planning as a team provides consistency across your grade as you work together to create engaging lessons. However, the Simply Stations Planning Tool can also be used individually if you're the only second-grade teacher in your school or if you want to try these ideas on your own first before working with a group.

Planning as a team will save time, over time. When you collaborate, your plans will be stronger. Someone may know children's literature well, another person may love to teach writing, and another team member may be good at creating visuals everyone can use. I've found that if you look carefully at your standards together, think about student needs, gather some good resources to model with, and put in the time to teach well, it pays off in the quality practice students do at the matching stations across the school year.

I like to divide my planning chart into four columns, as shown in the example that follows. Let's walk through the Simply Stations Planning Tool together.

TIME-SAVING TIP: Save the Simply Stations Planning Tool charts you've designed and use them as a starting point to plan together year after year.

- Column 1 is where we write our state standard in its entirety (so we don't skip parts we don't like). Use my timeless standards to get you started, and then fill in the language of your state standard to be precise. When teaching writing, use standards related to writing genres rather than writing process. Include writing process as part of your everyday modeling.

- In column 2, make a bulleted list of the academic vocabulary you want to use when teaching. This is the same vocabulary you'll want students to use when they're practicing in stations, too! You can include this language on conversation cards that kids use in whole group and eventually at the Writing station. Several conversation cards are included as printables on the companion website. Feel free to make your own, too, to reflect the academic vocabulary students should be using in *your* state or school system.

- Column 3 is where we jot down ideas for whole group teaching. Include model text titles, anchor chart ideas, lesson ideas, and conversation card ideas here. (You'll find many ideas for column 3 in this section of the book!)

- Finally, we take what we've taught in whole group (column 3) and draw an arrow to move it to column 4 (Partner Practice at Literacy Stations) along with the name of the station it fits into. You'll notice that whatever you've taught in whole group writing will transfer over time into the Writing station.

Here's an example of a Simply Stations Planning Tool created by a team. Note the Writing station ideas in column 4 and see how they grew first from the standard through planning instruction. Use this as a model, and feel free to make it your own!

TIME-SAVING TIP:
I've included many printables, anchor chart ideas, and text titles in this book and on the companion website to help you get started. As you get more comfortable with stations in your classroom, create some of your own and share them with others with the hashtag #simplystations.

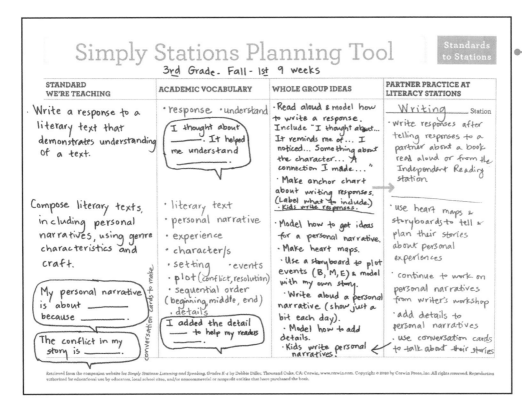

Simply Stations Planning Tool with four columns filled out by a team of third-grade teachers in Texas. They worked together to plan how to teach students to write responses and personal narratives early in the year and moved this work to the Writing station.

Teach *for* Transfer

From Whole Group to Stations

On the following pages, you'll find a number of Writing station ideas, all based on timeless literacy standards, to help you implement meaningful student practice. Remember, the timeless literacy standards I've included here are composites of standards encountered across states; wording may differ from the literacy standards used in your state or district, but you'll be able to find your exact standard that matches the timeless standard concept. In other words, these are meant to be a starting point. I hope you'll use the ideas in this section as a springboard for other engaging station work throughout the year.

Each sample lesson and accompanying station idea centers on a timeless literacy standard and includes the following information to help you get started:

WHAT IT IS: This breaks down what the standard means to clarify what we want learners to understand. I've included the most important information we want students to know deeply and be able to apply over writing multiple texts.

WHY IT'S IMPORTANT: It's important for both students *and* teachers to understand why we're learning something. In today's world, with all its distractions and competition for attention, it's especially important for students to understand the "why."

MYTHS AND CONFUSIONS: Because I've been teaching for more than four decades, I've worked through many misunderstandings and confusions children (and sometimes teachers) have around skills and standards. So, I'm laying these out at the start to help you be aware of problems that might occur and how to prevent them.

REAL-WORLD APPLICATIONS: This is sometimes referred to as "relevance." Children need to understand how they will be able to use this in the real world in order to help make their learning concrete and transferrable to other areas. This helps boost engagement, too.

You'll then find ideas for teaching for transfer in whole group and ways to move these concepts into station work for partners. I use the sequence of Plan, Teach, Practice, Reflect for each timeless standard:

1. **PLAN** thoughtfully (with your grade-level team if possible) to ensure student engagement and strong instruction. I've included sample texts to model with and key ideas to think about as you plan with a timeless standard in mind.

2. **TEACH** with intention. I've included sample anchor charts, conversation cards, graphic organizers, and tips to engage learners related to this timeless standard.

3. **PRACTICE** what's been taught at literacy stations (after students are familiar with the concept). Here you'll find grade-level adaptations for the timeless standard at this station and photos of what students at various ages can do at the Writing station.

4. **REFLECT** with your class. This will keep literacy stations going as students share what they're learning. It will give you a day-to-day pulse on student practice with "paperless accountability" as children share what they've done.

Photos throughout show you possibilities for what the Writing station can look like in your classroom, too.

TIMELESS WRITING STANDARDS

1.	The student will generate ideas, choose a topic, and make a plan that matches audience and purpose before writing.	Fiction/Nonfiction
2.	The student will write and revise stories with characters, sequenced events, and descriptive details.	Fiction
3.	The student will write and organize informational texts about topics of interest using text features and structures.	Nonfiction
4.	The student will write to express an opinion about a topic with reasons for support.	Nonfiction
5.	Students will peer edit for punctuation, capitalization, spelling, and language conventions.	Fiction/Nonfiction

Timeless Writing Standard 1

The student will generate ideas, choose a topic, and make a plan that matches audience and purpose before writing.

Let's examine this timeless standard before we begin teaching and moving it into a Writing station. By teaching this standard well, children will know how to choose their own ideas and plan for their writing. They will learn how to think about who will read their writing and why they are composing this piece. By practicing these same skills on their own or with a partner at the Writing station, learners will have the opportunity to continue to grow as writers.

Look closely at your own state standards for specific grade-level expectations and academic vocabulary. Most states focus on these skills as part of the writing process. This standard may include words like **first draft**, **brainstorming**, **plan**, **writing process**, or **prewriting**.

What It Is

- Writing starts with an idea, a topic, something the writer is interested in writing about!

- Writers plan what they will write. Some make outlines. Some jot down notes on paper. Others sketch or storyboard their ideas. Their writing might change throughout the process, but there is usually a plan to start with.

- Writers think about their audience before writing. They think

  ○ Who will read this? Why?

  ○ What will the reader want to know?

  ○ What do I want the reader to visualize or feel as they read?

- Before writing, writers in Grades K–4 may

  ○ Talk to someone about their ideas

○ Tell what they'll write before writing it down

○ Draw pictures to rehearse and plan their ideas

○ Use a graphic organizer to plan their writing

○ Think about their audience and purpose

Why It's Important

- Having a plan for what to write makes the writing clearer and easier to compose, especially for those who struggle with writing.

- If students are always given topics of what to write, they often have trouble coming up with their own ideas.

- Writing about something they know and care about gives students ownership of their writing.

- Thinking about audience and purpose strengthens writing and may increase motivation to write.

Myths and Confusions

- Giving students writing prompts is one option when teaching writing. On state tests children are given prompts, but that doesn't mean we must teach most writing through telling kids what to write every day. If students are always given prompts and story starters, they may have trouble coming up with their own ideas for writing.

- Using a formula for writing may help some students get started. But to really tap into student voice, it's important for children to select topics they know and care about.

- Free writing in journals is not writing instruction. It gives children a chance to write and may help them generate ideas of what to write about. But it should be coupled with models where the teacher writes and thinks aloud in front of the class on a variety of topics in a range of genres regularly.

- Having young writers in kindergarten and early first grade use a graphic organizer to plan their writing can be counterproductive. They will often try to write *everything* on the graphic organizer and then copy their words. This can frustrate them (and you!). Try having them draw pictures to rehearse their ideas and tell someone what they'll write as a plan.

- Be sure children understand *audience* when writing. If the audience is always the teacher, kids may not care much about what they write.

Expand audience to include their peers, family members, other classes, children's book authors, and community members, to name a few.

- Ditto for *purpose*. Authentic purpose is critical. Students should write for reasons beyond passing the state test or because my teacher said to write this.

Real-World Connections

- We use writing in everyday life. Think of the kinds of writing you do at work and beyond—emails, texts, lesson plans, notes, letters, lists, reports. You start with an idea before you write any of these, and you consider audience and purpose.

- We write for a variety of purposes—to send messages to friends and family, to communicate ideas with peers, to plan and remember things to do, to ask for assistance, to record what we've learned. Share your writing with students so they see how we use writing in our lives.

- Writing leaves lasting impressions, especially in online spaces. It's important to be thoughtful about our ideas, audience, and purpose to communicate clearly. Having a plan helps to structure and organize our writing.

How Practice at the Writing Station Helps Students

- Having a partner to talk to about what to write is motivating and can help kids come up with writing ideas.

- Talking to and making a writing plan with a partner is less overwhelming than doing this on your own.

- If students share with a partner what they will write about, tell who their audience is and why they are writing something, it may clarify their thinking and make their writing more focused.

It's important to teach concepts well in whole group before moving this work into the Writing station. This will help students to learn how to practice the same activities with a partner independent of you.

Start with helping kids generate ideas. Then move into having them choose a topic or idea. Finally model how to think about audience and purpose. Show different ways to plan for writing, too. Consider these steps for student success with this standard.

1. Plan

Select Picture Books for Model Texts

Because you'll use picture books for modeling and then place them in the Writing station, think about this standard and the kind of text that will help children understand what you want them to try. Start by choosing picture books that show how to generate ideas for writing. Over time, kids might reread these books or use them to get ideas at the Writing station.

Look for books like these to help students generate ideas, choose topics, and make plans for writing:

TIME-SAVING TIP:
Read aloud these books during reading time and then revisit them another day during writing. This will give kids more time to write during writing time!

KINDERGARTEN	GRADES 1–2	GRADES 3–4
• Books from guided reading that have a pattern and just one line of print per page	• *Rocket Writes a Story* by Tad Hill	• Wordless books geared to older students (*Flotsam* and others by David Wiesner; *Mirror* by Jeannie Baker; *Boat of Dreams* by Rogerio Coelho; *The Secret Box* and others by Barbara Lehman)
• Wordless picture books that show experiences young children are familiar with (e.g., *Good Dog, Carl* by Alexandra Day; *Good Night, Gorilla* by Peggy Rathmann)	• *My Map Book* by Sara Fanelli (see the page on Heart Maps)	
	• *Rufus the Writer* by Elizabeth Bram	
	• *I Wrote You a Note* by Lizi Boyd	• *The Whisper* by Pamela Zagarenski
• Simple picture books with repetition (*Hold Hands* by Sara Varon; *Ish* by Peter Reynolds)	• Question and answer books (*I Kissed the Baby* by Mary Murphy)	• *Chester's Masterpiece* by Mélanie Watt
	• *Any Questions?* by Marie-Louise Gay	• Informational texts about experiences students have had (*Our Very Own Dog* by Amanda McCardie)
• Books that use labels (*Warning! Do Not Touch!* by Tim Barnes; books by Todd Parr)	• Books in a series (like Pigeon or Elephant and Piggie)	
	• *Library Mouse* by Daniel Kirk	• *Amelia's Notebook* by Marissa Moss
• Picture dictionaries (*Scholastic First Picture Dictionary*; *DK First Picture Dictionary: Spanish*)	• *What Do You Do with an Idea?* by Kobi Yamada	

Select Topics for Modeled Writing or Write Aloud

Plan before you begin modeling writing. Think about topics you know and care a lot about. Share several ideas and think aloud about which you want to write about. For example, *I could write about my cat, Stripe. He was always getting in trouble at our house. Or maybe I'll write about going to the garden center and choosing flowers for my spring garden. I know! Last night my niece lost her front tooth and sent me a picture. She was so excited. I'd like to write about that to help me remember her delight!*

Also, keep in mind what you might do to plan your writing. Will you use a graphic organizer your kids will use, too? Or will you do a quick sketch first to organize your ideas? Will you use several pieces of paper stapled together to make a little book?

2. Teach

Co-Create Anchor Charts in Whole Group

Make an anchor chart *with* your class on how to get writing ideas. Also make charts on how to choose topics. Post these where children can easily see them during whole group instruction. Then move the charts (or mini versions of them) to the Writing station for reference. Here are some examples to get you started.

Anchor chart on how to come up with writing ideas from Grades K–1.

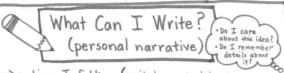

What Can I Write?
(personal narrative)

- Do I care about this idea?
- Do I remember details about it?

→ a time I felt... (excited, surprised, lonely, worried...)

→ special day (birthday, vacation, holiday...)

→ things I've done with my family

→ things I do with my friends

→ school memories

→ firsts (1st day I saw..., 1st tooth I lost...)

→ pets (funny times, loving moments...)

Anchor chart on generating writing ideas for upper grades

How to Pick an Idea

I like to fish.

BIG idea

small moment

Do I know... about it?

Do I care about it?

Anchor chart on how to choose a topic for writing from Grades K–1.

How to Narrow A Topic

Who will read this?

What do I know about?

What do I care about?

① Start with a BIG idea.

going to the mountains

② Narrow it down.

camping in a tent

③ Think of <u>one</u> <u>event</u> that is important to you!

rainstorm at night in the tent

Why am I writing this?

What will my readers want to know?

Anchor chart on how to narrow a topic for writing in upper grades.

TIME-SAVING TIP:
Consider taking a photo of the finished anchor chart, then printing it in a smaller size to post at the Writing station.

Model How to Make an Idea Map

Making idea maps is one way to brainstorm before writing. Idea maps should be updated periodically to keep them fresh. Kids return to their idea maps for inspiration when they're not sure what to write about. Here are several ideas for idea maps you can turn to throughout the year.

- Heart maps: Students fill in a heart shape with names of people they love, places they know, things they like to do, special celebrations, favorites, and so on.

- Bone maps: This is a place where they write down ideas that are "close to their bones." This might be a cooler option for older kids who think hearts are too feminine. They write similar ideas, just in a different shape.

- Brain maps: Try a picture of a blank head where students jot down "things on my mind."

- Territory maps: Start by thinking about a place you love, like the beach or a forest or your grandma's attic. Then sketch ideas in that place.

- Create-your-own maps: Once students know how to make idea maps, let them play with creating any shape they want for their map. For example, someone who loves to sing might draw a large musical note, a soccer lover might draw a big soccer ball with ideas inside it, or a kid infatuated by dinosaurs might jot down ideas inside a large T. rex.

I've included sample lessons for modeling at the end of this section to help you get started. Map templates can be found at the companion website at **resources .corwin.com/simplystations-writing**.

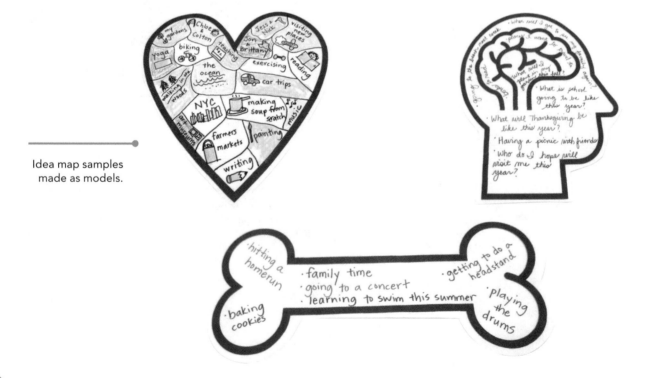

Idea map samples made as models.

Create a Community Journal of Ideas to Place at the Writing Station

As a class you might keep an ongoing list of things everybody knows about from their collective experiences at school. Keep these in a Community Journal, a spiral notebook the whole class uses for ideas. You could divide it into sections marked with sticky note labels, such as *favorite lines from read alouds, characters we love, science topics studied, social studies topics studied, places we've visited together, people we've met as a class.*

Add to the Community Journal *with* your class during whole group instruction by gluing in a photo or jotting down a few words. For example, in the Characters We Love section glue a picture of a character from a read aloud book and jot down words around it from the book that describe that character. Students may use this character or adapt it to create their own in a story. Likewise, jot down a science topic studied with key vocabulary words and matching pictures (kids can draw) to refer to when writing informational text. See the example on the right.

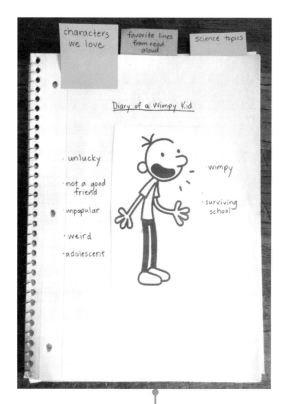

Pages from a Community Journal to use for ideas at the Writing station.

Model how to use the Community Journal when writing with your class. Then move it to the Writing station for students to use for ideas, too.

Model How to Use a Writer's Notebook for Ideas

A writer's notebook is another place where students can keep ideas for writing, as well as sketch out writing plans. Each student decorates the front of a spiral or composition book with pictures found online or in a magazine that reflect their lives and interests. Kids can use writer's notebooks to jot down

- Interesting words and phrases from independent reading books
- Lists of favorites
- Anecdotes of funny things that happened in class or at home
- Snippets of conversation overheard
- Possible titles of pieces to write
- Story beginning or ending lines
- Sketches of places they've seen or characters they know or imagine
- Quick writes

I create my own writer's notebook as a seedbed for each new book I write. In it I jot down ideas, note titles of picture books to teach with, and record questions teachers ask me in workshops. Here are a few photos of writer's notebooks.

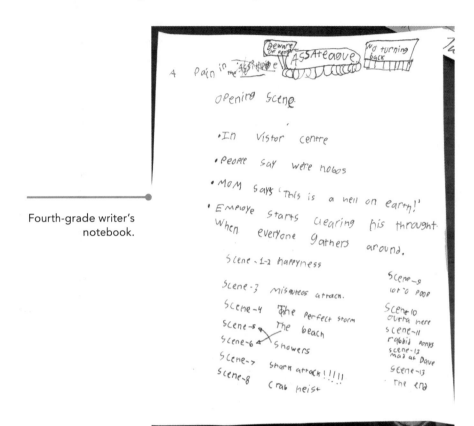

Fourth-grade writer's notebook.

Pages from my current writer's notebook.

Try Quick Writes

Quick writes are different from simply writing in a journal. First, they're short and timed. Set a visible timer for two to three minutes and have kids write in their notebooks or on plain paper while you do the same.

When the timer goes off, have a brief sharing time. Ask a few students to read aloud their writing. Or have them share with partners or small groups. The purpose is to get them started as writers and help them think of ideas. Instead of giving kids a boring prompt, try one of these ideas.

- Give one word related to a topic of interest or study (butterfly, magnet, pizza, bike).

- Read a line from a favorite read-aloud or poem (*Not a hotdog, my hotdog*).

- Ask, "Would you rather ___ or ___?" (play soccer or read a book).

- Share an interesting piece of art.

- Show a funny picture.

EL TIP: Use a picture card with the word printed below for quick writes.

Use Simple Graphic Organizers to Help Students Plan Their Writing

Familiar graphic organizers from reading may also be used in writing to help students plan, especially in grades two through four. Consider using a circle map, a web, or a tree map. Model with these first. Show how to jot down words and phrases, not sentences, so kids don't write their whole piece in the graphic organizer! Also, model how to use the ideas in the graphic organizer to start writing a piece.

It might be fun to show students samples of plans writers use. Here are a few to get you started:

- J.K. Rowling's notes when planning Harry Potter books: https://bit.ly/2FYvPrP

- Here are sample sketches and plans from Andrea Prior: https://bit.ly/2W7HvO3

- A page from Mo Willems' sketchbook: https://bit.ly/32390Mm

- Notes from Eric Carle about his process: https://bit.ly/2Ocdk3T

For kids in kindergarten and early first grade, you might use simple paper with space for a picture and a few lines for writing. I like to give children three pieces: one for the beginning, another for the middle, and a third for the end. Have them draw a picture on each page to show who, where, and what is happening. Then have them tell their story or information to go with each page. Finally, have kids write words to go with their drawings. See the online companion at **resources.corwin.com/simplystations-writing** for a printable of primary grade paper. You might print some on light green paper, some on pale yellow, and some on pink (for beginning, middle, and end). Kids can even staple them together to make a book when done.

B-	M-	E-
• Kelly was **scared**, because she might swallow her loose tooth. • Before bedtime.	• Bedtime. • She had trouble falling asleep. • She listed to music 2x. • She asked for water 2x. • She sneaked downstairs and went in the backyard, but mosquitoes chased her. • She feel asleep. • Kelly's tooth fell out and felt **weird in her mouth** in the morning.	• She felt **excited**. • She went to her mom and dad's room. • She put her tooth under her pillow for the tooth fairy.

Student uses a graphic organizer for beginning, middle, and end to plan her writing.

Beginning, middle, and end paper used by kids to make books in Grades K–2.

Try Digital Tools for Planning What to Write

Becoming a writer in today's digital age may differ from the experiences we had as writers in school. Take advantage of digital tools to help kids plan and keep track of what they write. See Section 4 for a list of some to try.

Word clouds can be used to generate ideas for student writing.

Created via wordclouds.com

Use Conversation Cards to Develop Accountable Talk

Model how to talk about ideas, audience, and purpose before writing. Conversation cards may prompt students to use academic vocabulary as they talk with others. Use these cards in whole group (and small group) to teach student expectations. Eventually, you'll move these cards to the Writing station for students to use as they work together. (There are printable conversation cards found on the online companion that look like the thumbnails below.)

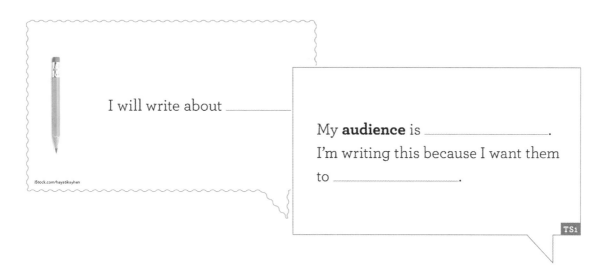

On the following pages are two sample lessons for modeling that you can use when teaching children about generating ideas during whole group instruction. One lesson is for primary grades and focuses on generating ideas; the other is for intermediate learners making a plan for writing. Please use these as examples to get you started with strong whole group lessons that will then be transferred to partner practice at the Writing station. Use model texts in read-aloud during your reading block. Then use them again during writing instruction (but not necessarily the same day). Reading aloud and sharing books for different purposes will save time throughout the day. Teach these lessons more than once and watch children become more proficient at generating ideas and planning their writing. Substitute different text as you teach the lessons multiple times.

SAMPLE WRITING LESSON WITH A MODEL TEXT in PRIMARY GRADES

MODEL TEXT: *Ralph Tells a Story* by Abby Hanlon (picture book that talks about ideas in writing)

TIMELESS STANDARD: The student will generate ideas before writing. (Note that I'm intentionally focusing on just part of the timeless standard, which is something you can do, too. Just adjust it to match your state/district standards.)

TEACHER TALK:

- Writing starts with an idea.

- Ideas come from all around us. Pay attention to people you see, places you go, and things that make you smile.

- When you get an idea for writing, tell somebody! Or make a quick sketch so you don't forget. I like to use sticky notes to keep track of my writing ideas.

- Looking at a picture can give you a writing idea, too.

STUDENT TALK: Use the conversation card to demonstrate. Kids will use these in whole group and at the Writing station, too. (Download printable conversation cards from the online companion, **resources .corwin.com/simplystations-writing**.)

- I will write about _____.

- My **idea** is _____.

LESSON STEPS:

Teach this lesson across several days to keep students engaged.

1. Read aloud the story, inviting children to enjoy it and think about how Ralph got ideas for his story. Jot down some of their ideas. See the following sample from a kindergarten classroom.

2. The next day, review your idea list. Then model how you think about an idea for your own writing. Share things about your life that might interest your class: *Our new puppy whined all night. I saw a deer in my backyard. My daughter lost her tooth.*

3. Use the same paper you want your students to use as you write aloud in front of the class. See my sample writing on the next page.

4. Have students talk to a partner about an idea they want to write about and then plan their stories by sketching on the paper you used for modeling.

5. The following day, show how to take your ideas and add writing. Then ask students to do the same.

Sample ideas list from kindergarten following read aloud of *Ralph Tells a Story*.

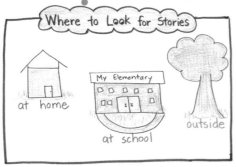

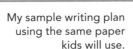

My sample writing plan using the same paper kids will use.

EL TIP: Multilingual students can draw first and then tell their writing plan.

QUICK ASSESS:

Could students generate ideas for writing? Can they tell a story using their ideas? Can they draw pictures to match their story as a plan?

AUTHOR'S CRAFT CONNECTION:

Use author's craft cards to help students think like writers. The goal is for students to understand this well enough that they can do this without teacher assistance at the Writing station. After they read, have them use these to discuss author's craft. (You can download printables from the online companion.)

- How did the author show Ralph's problem? (*pictures of his face, bold words, words in italics*)

- Look at how the author used speech bubbles. What do they tell the reader?

- What ideas does this book give you for writing a story? Show the part that gave you an idea.

READING CONNECTION:

Use this book during whole group reading instruction to talk about story elements. Have students identify the main character, the setting, the conflict, and the resolution. You might use a paper with three sections noting beginning, middle, and end for kids to record these elements. They'd jot the main characters and setting in the beginning, the conflict in the middle, and the resolution in the end. This could be used as a simple story writing plan, too. You can find a printable Story Writing Plan on the online companion at **resources.corwin .com/simplystations-writing**.

MOVING THIS LESSON TO PARTNER PRACTICE AT A STATION:

At the Writing station, have kids work with another student to brainstorm ideas (or use an idea list they've generated). They should talk about their ideas before writing and use planning paper to sketch out the beginning, middle, and end of their stories. Then they should write their stories. See Timeless Writing Standard 2 for more ideas on story writing. Have a place for them to store unfinished writing that they can return to when they visit the Writing station again. Provide author's craft cards, too, for them to use to talk about what the author did that they might try when they write.

SAMPLE WRITING LESSON WITH A MODEL TEXT in INTERMEDIATE GRADES

MODEL TEXT: *You Have to Write* by Janet Wong (a picture book for upper grades that addresses getting ideas for writing)

TIMELESS STANDARD: The student will generate ideas, choose a topic, and make a plan that matches audience and purpose before writing. (Be sure this reflects your state and grade-level standards; adjust accordingly.)

TEACHER TALK:

- Think of an idea for writing, something you know about and care about.

- Choose a topic by narrowing it down. Think of the part that readers would want to know about.

- Think about your audience. Who will read this?

- Think about your purpose for writing. Why are you writing this piece? What do you want your reader to know, understand, think, or feel?

- Plan your writing by organizing your ideas.

STUDENT TALK: Use conversation card printables from the online companion, **resources.corwin.com/simplystations-writing**. Kids will use these at the Writing station, too.

- I'm going to write about _____ because _____.

- My **topic** is _____. I narrowed it down to focus on _____.

- My **audience** is _____. I'm writing this because I want them to _____.

- I'm **planning** my writing by _____.

LESSON STEPS:

The goal is for students to talk with a partner about an idea, narrow the topic, and consider audience and purpose before writing. Then have them write their ideas down and organize these into a first draft. Over time, they will work on revising and editing. Once they understand how to make a plan, they can continue to practice without adult assistance at the Writing station.

1. Tell students they will learn about planning to write. Make an anchor chart of what to do before writing. See page 59 for ideas.

2. Before reading aloud the book, tell your class to pay attention to what the author tells us about looking for a writing idea, narrowing the topic, and organizing our words.

3. Read the book, stopping periodically to ask students what they noticed about where they might get ideas. Were the ideas about big events or just small things that happened in everyday life? Jot some examples listing big events and related, narrower topics, as shown on the next page.

4. Discuss different ways to organize their words, using the book as a reference. For example, write ideas on paper, lay the papers in a row, and cut and paste pieces.

5. The next day, review and begin to model how to do the things the author talked about in the book. Then have students do the same. Start with just talking about ideas, using a writer's

EL TIP: Talking before they write will help multilingual learners rehearse and organize their ideas.

notebook, and using a map, such as the heart map, bone map, or brain map. Printable versions are available online at **resources.corwin.com/simplystations-writing**.

Chart made with third graders listing big events and related narrower topics is used to plan writing.

Two students talk together at the Writing station to plan their writing.

Photo by Matthew Rood

QUICK ASSESS:

Were students able to generate and narrow their writing ideas? Did they think about audience and purpose? How did they plan their writing (e.g., making a sketch, using a graphic organizer)?

AUTHOR'S CRAFT CONNECTION:

Look back at the book to examine author's craft. Tell students that Janet Wong is a poet. Have them talk about what she did as a writer using the prompts below. The goal is for students to do this well enough so they can repeat this same kind of thinking at the Writing station to examine other books that might stimulate their writing with a classmate. Use author's craft cards to guide and support student talk. (A printable card for kids to use at the station is found on the companion site.)

- What form did the author use to write? (e.g., poem with stanzas)

- Look at the author's use of punctuation, especially questions. How can questions help you as a writer?

- Examine the illustrations. What ideas do they give you as a writer?

READING CONNECTION:

Use this book as a whole group read-aloud when you are teaching students to read poetry, too. Help them read, one stanza at a time, and talk about what they're visualizing. They might jot down words and phrases in their writer's notebooks that helped them picture something. These might be seeds for writing their own poems over time.

MOVING THIS LESSON TO PARTNER PRACTICE AT A STATION:

At the Writing station, have kids work with a partner using the same conversation cards from the lesson and planning sheets to jot down their ideas, including topic, audience, and purpose, but only after they show understanding of how to do this. They will definitely need multiple models! Have students take a photo of their finished plan to share with the class.

3. Partner Practice

Once you see that students can generate ideas and plan their writing, considering audience and purpose, you're ready to move that same work into partner practice at the Writing station. At first, learners will be doing much the same thing you've modeled during Launch Lessons. But over time, students should be able to extend this skill as they plan to write a wider variety of texts. Here are some additional, grade-specific suggestions to help you think about the best things for you to model and for your children to practice as they generate ideas, choose topics, and plan their writing at the Writing station.

Kindergarten

- Young students might use their heart maps for writing ideas if you've made these during writing time. If they have writing folders, glue their heart maps to the inside cover and store these folders in crates at your Writing station.

- Take photos of things your class does (e.g., playing outdoors, making projects, reading a story, going on a field trip, eating lunch) and display these on a board near your Writing station. These pictures may give them ideas of things to write about.

- Send an email or letter to families asking them to help their child choose several photos that they could write about at the Writing station. Students can keep these snapshots in their writing folders to generate ideas, too.

- Create small charts to place at the Writing station with words related to topics you've studied in social studies, science, or holidays/seasons.

These can help kids come up with ideas. Model with these in whole group first. Sample Grades K–1 Word Banks can be found below and on the online companion at **resources.corwin.com/simplystations-writing**.

Kindergartners use word charts to generate writing ideas during whole group writing time and at the Writing station.

Young writers use resources taught during whole group writing to plan at the Writing station.

Grades 1–2

- Use ideas listed for kindergarten above with first and second graders, as well. Let them use idea maps, as described on page 60 of this book.

- First and second graders love series books. It's okay for them to write a series, too. They might use the same characters in more than one book, which makes generating ideas a bit easier.

- Generating writing ideas takes a lot of practice, even for an experienced author! Students will work with this standard all year long. Periodically change out photos, writing genres, or word cards to help kids continue to come up with ideas for writing.

Grades 3–4

- Students at these grade levels may use graphic organizers to plan their writing. Stick with a few that you've modeled with well. Place blank graphic organizers in clear plastic sleeves to go with a genre of writing on your display area.

- Include a Community Journal (a spiral notebook shared by the class) for kids to use as a seedbed for ideas at the Writing station.

- Post heart maps, bone maps, or other idea maps at your Writing station to remind students to use these to generate ideas.

Upper grade students generate ideas together at the Writing station.

4. Reflect With Students

After your students have worked with this timeless standard at the Writing station, reflect on what they've done here. Be sure to include a five- to ten-minute Reflection Time after stations where children can tell others what they've learned and done at this station. You might also refer to Section 4 in this book and the online companion to jot down your ideas about the work you and your children did. If they took photos of their writing plans, have them project these to share with the class.

Students may use the questions below to talk about the work that they did at the Writing station during cleanup time. During Reflection Time, you can ask these questions again to learn more about what students did at this station today. (There are matching printables on the companion website, **resources .corwin.com/simplystations-writing**, that you can place at the Writing station for readers to use.)

1. What did you write about at the Writing station today? How did you come up with your idea?

2. How did you plan your writing at the Writing station today? What did you use to get started?

3. Who was your audience for what you wrote today? Why did you write this piece?

Timeless Writing Standard 2

> **The student will write and revise stories with characters, sequenced events, and descriptive details.**

Let's take a look at this timeless standard before we begin teaching and moving it into a Writing station. Look closely at your own state standards for grade-level expectations and academic vocabulary. By teaching students how to write and revise stories with interesting characters, events in logical order, and descriptive details, they may create well-written pieces for others to read. By practicing at a Writing station, learners will have the opportunity to continue honing their craft as story writers.

What It Is

- Stories can be personal narratives (about things that really happened) or fiction (made up stories) or a combination of both.

- Writing a story involves understanding how to weave together story elements, including

  - Characters: Just a few that may have an adventure together

  - Setting: When and where the story takes place that affects characters' interactions

  - Conflict: A problem that logically might occur based on the characters and their adventures

  - Resolution: How the characters work together to solve the problem

- Stories should have events sequenced in logical order, including the following

  - Beginning: Characters and setting introduced

  - Middle: Conflict or a problem that needs fixing takes place here

  - End: Resolution occurs

- Details help the reader envision characters, setting, and the events in a story and may include

  - Specific names of people and places

  - Words that evoke sensory images (how things look, sound, smell, taste, feel)

  - Dialogue or conversation between characters that sounds like real people and moves the action forward

Why It's Important

- Stories are powerful. They help us relate to each other. They can help us take action or change our thinking.

- Writing a story helps students learn to organize their thoughts and tell others what they've lived through or imagined.

- Structuring a story from beginning to end gives children the opportunity to apply story elements they've learned about as readers.

- As we write stories, we use our powers of creativity and imagination.

Myths and Confusions

- Young children often write "bed-to-bed" stories that just list events that happen from the beginning of the day to the end. Kids may write, *I got up and brushed my teeth. Then I had breakfast. Then I went to school. After school, I went home. Then I had dinner and went to sleep.* These stories need interesting characters and events.

- Students sometimes try to put too much dialogue in their stories, especially when they first learn about using quotation marks. Help them look at how authors of books they enjoy use conversation. Also examine how dialogue helps the story move forward.

- Sometimes kids just want to retell TV shows or movies they've seen. Or they want to tell about video games they've played. This is a starting point for some children, but it can limit their creativity. Try to help students expand their writing beyond these somewhat passive experiences. Encourage them to craft stories about their families, friends, and more active experiences (e.g., playing a sport, taking a walk, describing something special). This will help them develop voice, especially if you expand their sense of audience beyond the teacher. If some children are persistent in writing about TV shows, movies, or video games, help them use characters they know to create new adventures.

Real-World Connections

- Stories are part of our everyday lives. We tell each other about people we have met or worked with, we share sequenced events of things we have experienced, and we provide descriptive details about those people and events.

- Characters from stories we have read or watched influence the stories we tell and write.

- Storytelling is useful in many creative occupations that kids may have interest in, such as journalism, moviemaking, and even video game creation.

- Social media encourages the use of storytelling to build a brand, sell ideas, and influence thinking.

- Stories have been passed along in the oral tradition for many, many years all over the world. The stories we tell teach lessons and preserve cultures and traditions. Families share stories about their childhoods and departed relatives their children may never have met to keep those memories alive.

How Practice at the Writing Station Helps Students

- As children write their stories, they better understand how stories work. They have the chance to apply what they understand about story elements as they use these in their writing.

- Partners can help each other with their writing. They can bounce ideas off each other. They can tell and write stories together. They can listen to each other's writing and give constructive feedback. They can use examples from model texts for assistance.

- Students can use familiar writing tools at the writing station. They can use graphic organizers, model texts, and vocabulary from stories as they write their own.

- Talking about what they wrote with a partner can strengthen student writing.

EL TIP: Ask children to tell their stories first before writing. Multilingual students might use photos or illustrations to help. Record the stories and allow students to listen to their stories. Listening may encourage them to talk more.

It's important to teach concepts well in whole group before moving this work into the Writing station. This will help students eventually know how to practice the same activities with a partner independent of you. Consider the following steps for whole group instruction to ensure student success with this standard.

1. Plan

Select Picture Books With Interesting Characters, Sequenced Story Events, and Descriptive Details

Because you'll be modeling the writing work kids will do in the Writing station, think about your students, this standard, and the kinds of texts that will help them compose their own stories. Look for fiction books with characters children enjoy and connect to. Find stories with characters who have experiences similar to those of your students. This will help them tap into their own lives to think of stories they could tell. Also look for picture books about children who are trying to write stories. These books may help kids overcome obstacles to writing.

Here are some things to look for when choosing books to model with during writing time and for students to use at the Writing station. (A list with some recommended titles is included in Section 4, too.)

KINDERGARTEN	GRADES 1–2	GRADES 3–4
• Short texts with one or two main characters that do things kinder-gartners do (get in trouble, talk too much, have wiggly teeth, make friends)	• Stories about little kids writing their own stories or making their own books	• Picture books with strong characters that kids can relate to
• Stories about families, classmates, or friends	• Favorite books in a series (characters repeat but settings or conflicts may change)	• Short chapter books, especially those in a series
• Settings familiar to five- and six-year-olds (home, school, park, zoo, farm, store)	• Books with dialogue on some pages	• Graphic novels
• Short conversations in speech bubbles	• Story books with short chapters	• Books about authors and illustrators (that tell about their craft)
• Limited print on a page	• Folk and fairy tales	• Short stories from children's magazines
	• Short stories from children's magazines	• More dialogue that helps advance the action and tells about characters

Think Ahead About Characters, Settings, Conflicts, and Resolutions for Modeled Writing or Write Aloud

Plan ahead what you might write about as you model in front of students. Think about a character or two you might include in your story. You might even choose one from a favorite read aloud book! Likewise think about setting.

Where and when might this character's actions logically take place? What's a problem your character might have? Choose something your students can relate to. And then think ahead about the resolution.

You might have a graphic organizer ready where you can jot down your ideas just like you'll want your kids to do. Plan ahead but be flexible when you begin to compose your story in front of your class. Sometimes writers change their minds as they begin to write stories, and it's great to model this.

Plan Which Writing Tools You'll Use

Since you're going to have kids write stories, it's a good idea to prepare pre-stapled booklets ahead of time. For Grades K–2 students, I like to use green paper for the beginning, yellow for the middle, and pink for the end. You might also provide white paper for covers. Model writing with the same paper you're going to have children use. You might have some unlined and some with boxes and lines.

Older students might like to use notebook paper. Or they may enjoy writing sequenced stories using comic strip paper. A variety of paper printables for children at different ages and stages can be found in the online companion.

Likewise, think about what you will write with: a pencil or dark pen. Will you use colored pencils, crayons, or markers to add illustrations?

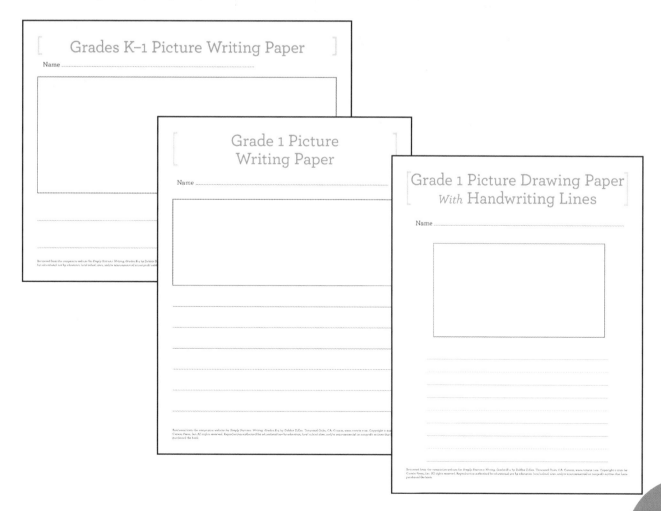

2. Teach

Model in Whole Group Write Aloud

During writing time it's important to show kids *how* to write a story. Think aloud as you write the beginning of your story. Show the class your plan for characters and setting. Then start to write a bit as they watch. You might use a model text (read aloud previously so it's familiar) and refer to something the author did that you'd like to try. See the model lessons in this section for ideas.

Debbie writes a story in front of a kindergarten class to model what they are expected to do.

Start With Sequencing Events

For beginning writers, you might use simple sequencing cards that they can put in order to tell a story before writing. Limit it to four or five cards. You might use pictures from children's magazines (print or online). Work with kids to put the cards in sequential order and tell a story with a beginning, middle, and end. Then help them write the words.

For older students, you might use a short story from a children's magazine (print or online). Cut it apart into a beginning chunk, several middle parts, and an ending section. Then have students read it with you and put the pieces in order sequentially. Think aloud about the beginning, middle, and ending.

Simple sequencing cards put in order to help kids tell and then write a story.

Beginning, middle, and ending events from a short story reassembled by kids to help them understand sequential order before writing their own stories.

Fill in the Middle of a Story

If you're showing students how to write a story, you might have the beginning and end already written on pages for a little book or on a graphic organizer. You could use beginnings and endings from folk tales or familiar books. Or use events from students' lives (e.g., *My tooth was loose. My baby brother cried all night. I thought he was my friend.*) Work together to think about and sequence events in the middle. See the lesson for Grades K–1 in this section for ideas.

Co-Create Anchor Charts to Remind Students What to Try as Story Writers

Make an anchor chart (or several) about writing a story. One might list story elements to include in your writing. Another chart could go into detail about creating a character who readers can connect to. A third anchor chart might refer to how to include conversation in your story. See samples on the next page to get you started.

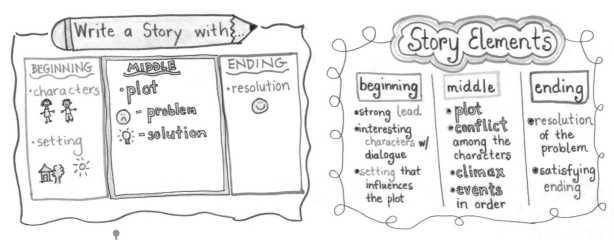

Write a Story with...

BEGINNING	MIDDLE	ENDING
• characters	• plot	• resolution
• setting	☹ - problem	☺
	💡 - solution	

Story Elements

beginning	middle	ending
• strong lead	• plot	• resolution of the problem
• interesting characters w/ dialogue	• conflict among the characters	• satisfying ending
• setting that influences the plot	• climax	
	• events in order	

Sample anchor charts list story elements to include when writing. The one on the left was made in primary grades; the one on the right is from intermediate.

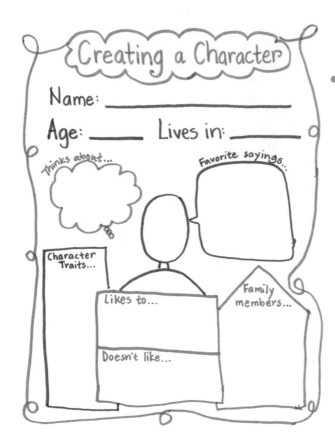

Creating a Character

Name: _____

Age: _____ Lives in: _____

Thinks about...

Favorite sayings...

Character Traits...

Likes to...

Doesn't like...

Family members...

This anchor chart was made in second grade to help students think about creating characters.

Using "Dialogue" in a Story

Think about...
The character _____
talking to _____
about _____.
Their moods are _____.

"What's the matter?" Mama asked.

"In America I have lost my name."

• Keep it short.
• Read it aloud to see how it sounds.
• Does it tell about the characters?
• Does it show a conflict?
• If you can remove it, you didn't need it!

An anchor chart made in fourth grade helps kids consider how to use conversation in their stories.

Add Details to Make a Story Come to Life

Write a simple story ahead of time and share it with your students on chart paper or a projection device. Read it together and model how to add details to make it more interesting. Show kids how to think aloud about questions you have as a reader. For example, as you read a child's story about fishing, ask *"Where did you go fishing? What was the weather like that day? How did you feel? Why?"*

You might also ask students for permission to use their stories in a similar way. Have the student writer use the pen to add details in front of the class in response to questions.

On the following pages are two sample lessons for modeling that you can use when teaching children about writing their own stories during whole group instruction. One lesson is for primary grades and focuses on how to write a story and sequence events using a beginning, middle, and ending; the other is for intermediate learners showing them how to revise stories by adding descriptive details that bring characters and their problems to life. Please use these as examples to get you started with strong whole group lessons that will then be transferred to partner practice at the Writing station.

Read aloud books during your reading block that will become model texts to use again during writing instruction (but not necessarily the same day). Teach these lessons more than once and watch children become more proficient at writing their own stories with interesting characters, sequenced events, and descriptive details. Substitute different text as you teach the lessons multiple times. Write aloud more than one of your own stories with your class. Use events from your own life. Model, model, model!

SAMPLE WRITING LESSON WITH A MODEL TEXT in PRIMARY GRADES

MODEL TEXT: *One Day, The End: Short, Very Short, Shorter-Than-Ever Stories* by Rebecca Kai Dotlich (short picture book without many words to help children tell stories)

TIMELESS STANDARD: The student will write and revise stories with characters, sequenced events, and descriptive details. (Be sure this reflects your state and grade-level standards.)

TEACHER TALK:

- Things happen in order in a story just like in real life.

- Think about the beginning of this story.

- What happened in the middle of this story? What was the problem or conflict? How was the problem solved?

- How did the author end the story? Think about your story's ending, too.

STUDENT TALK: Use matching printables found on the companion site. Kids may use these at the Writing station, too.

- My story is **in order. First . . . then . . . next . . . at the end . . . .**

- My story **starts** with the words _____.

- My story **ends** with the words _____.

LESSON STEPS:

1. Read aloud the book one day. On another day, return to this book during Writing Workshop. Read aloud the first page. Have students name the three parts of a story (beginning, middle, end).

2. Choose an idea from the book to help them tell a story. (This book has several.) Ahead of time, write the beginning on a piece of paper (e.g., *One day I went to school.*) and the end on another (e.g., *I came home.*) Add a simple drawing on each page.

3. Have students think about what might happen in the middle. They can use the book for ideas. Have them turn and talk to a partner about the middle of this story.

4. Ask a few kids to share their ideas with the class. Model how to draw and write a bit of what might happen in the middle of the story on a third page. Think aloud about the importance of putting the events in the order they would really happen. Then put these three pages in order and staple them.

5. Tell students they will write their own stories with a beginning, middle, and end. They can use the same beginning as the book or make up their own. Give them each three pieces of paper and have them work on their beginning page.

6. Confer with students individually as they write independently. Help them think about what would happen in order and add details.

7. After they've written for a bit (five to fifteen minutes), meet as a group and have one or two students share their writing. The class might ask questions or tell what they pictured in their minds.

8. Have students continue working on their stories for several days. Model how to read what they've written, think, and then write some more. Model this with your own writing, too. Show how to make your words and pictures match the events in order.

QUICK ASSESS:

Did children tell and write a story with a clear beginning, middle, and end? Were the events in order? Did the pictures and words match?

AUTHOR'S CRAFT CONNECTION:

Use author's craft cards to help students. A printable can be found in the online companion. The goal is for students eventually to understand how to think about how authors begin and end stories well enough that they can continue to do this without teacher assistance at the Writing station. Remind young readers to look at the illustrations and words.

- The author used the words _____ to start the story.

- The author used the words _____ to end the story.

READING CONNECTION:

This book has very simple stories. Have kids read and then tell the beginning, middle, and end of other stories they read. They might use the retelling strip found in *Simply Stations: Partner Reading.* Or use retelling pieces to help them retell familiar stories.

MOVING THIS LESSON TO PARTNER PRACTICE AT A STATION:

At the Writing station, have kids work with a partner to tell stories with a beginning, middle, and end. They might work together to write a story and add details. They may use pictures from the model text to help them come up with a beginning and end. Or they might write a story on their own and then share it with their partner. Provide the conversation cards, anchor charts, and author's craft cards for them to use. You might also add picture cards for them to sequence and use to generate their own stories.

EL TIP: Have preprinted pages with a simple beginning (e.g., *One day I made something.*) and ending (e.g., *I gave it to Mom.*) like those in the model text. Help multilingual students tell what happens in between and draw/write it on a blank page or two to go in the middle. Then staple the pages together to make a little book.

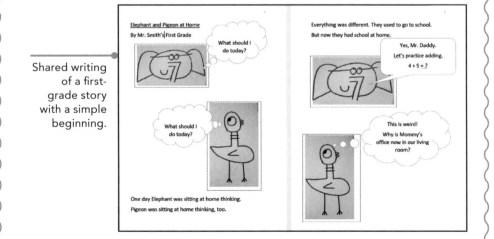

Shared writing of a first-grade story with a simple beginning.

SAMPLE WRITING LESSON WITH A MODEL TEXT in INTERMEDIATE GRADES

MODEL TEXTS: *The Best Story* by Eileen Spinelli (a story about a character that had trouble writing a story); or a picture book with characters, sequenced events, and descriptive details for older students

TIMELESS STANDARD: The student will write and revise stories with characters, sequenced events, and descriptive details. (Be sure this reflects your state and grade-level standards for language arts.)

TEACHER TALK:

- Authors write their stories and then revise them.

- It's okay to change your story after you write it the first time.

- Write your story and then read it out loud again. Think about the details that will help the reader understand your characters and their feelings, motivations, and actions.

- Be sure your story's events are in the order they would really happen.

STUDENT TALK: Use matching printables found on the companion website. Kids will use these at the Writing Station, too.

- I added the **detail** _____ to help my readers _____.

- I **revised** my story to make the part about _____ clearer.

- When I read my story aloud, I realized I'd forgotten to include _____.

- When I read my story aloud, I took out (or moved) this part, because it didn't make sense: _____.

LESSON STEPS:

1. Read aloud the book one day. On another day, return to this book during Writing Workshop. Talk about the main character's problem (e.g., She had trouble thinking about events to put in her story.).

2. Ask students to make connections to this story. Help them understand that writers revise, or make changes, to their stories. This is what writers do! Discuss some of the ways the main character changed her story and what she finally decided. Look at details the author used to describe this

character (e.g., *my favorite author who wrote a book about roller coasters; I sharpened five pencils; opened my notebook to a brand-new page*).

3. Then show students the beginning of a story you wrote ahead of time. (Write it quickly and don't add too much detail, just like your students might.) Project it and ask them to read it aloud with you. Invite them to ask questions if they want more details about the character or stop you if something seems out of order or doesn't make sense. Briefly model how to draw a carat to add a detail or a line to delete or an arrow to move parts.

4. Have students work on their own stories. They might start a new one or reread a story they've already written. Remind them to think about details that might help the reader picture and understand their characters. Tell them it's okay to move story events around to make sense.

5. As students write on their own, confer with them individually. Use the Teacher Talk suggestions to help them add descriptive details and sequence events.

6. After independent writing (about fifteen to twenty minutes), meet as a class and have one or two students share their writing. Others might ask questions or give suggestions to help the writer revise.

7. Have students continue to write their stories over several days. Continue to model how to think, then write, then read. Use your own writing. Or invite a student to do this in front of the class.

QUICK ASSESS:

Did students think, write, and then read their stories aloud to themselves? Did they revise their stories by putting events in sequential order or removing parts that didn't make sense? Did children add descriptive details to make their characters come alive?

AUTHOR'S CRAFT CONNECTION:

Use author's craft cards to help students pay attention to how authors add descriptive details to their stories. (A printable can be found in the online companion.) The goal is for students eventually to understand how to do this well enough that they can continue without teacher assistance in their own stories at the Writing station.

Model how to first read aloud a page from a story. Then use sticky notes cut into skinny pieces to cover up descriptive words in the text. Now read it aloud without the details. As you uncover the words, pay attention to what kinds of things the author added as details (e.g., proper nouns, adjectives, words that tell more). You might list examples on a chart. See the photo below.

- Choose a page. Find descriptive details the author used. Cover them with sticky notes. Read the story. How does it sound?

- Find descriptive words in the story that tell when something happened. What does this help you picture?

- Find details in the story that tell where something happened. What do you see in your mind?

- Look for adjectives on a page. What do they help you better picture? Does every sentence have them?

EL TIP: Have students look at an illustration in the book and tell about details they notice using sentences. This may help them later find and use descriptive details in the texts they read and write.

Chart about descriptive details the author added in the model text *The Best Story*.

3. Partner Practice

Include writing stories as an option at the Writing station after you see that students know how to write stories with characters, sequenced events, and/or descriptive details. Provide model texts, anchor charts, and other supports to help them practice what you've taught them to try as story writers. After they've learned about revising, move this work into the Writing station, too. Again, provide samples and charts at the station for support. Here are some additional, grade-level specific suggestions to help you think about the best things for children to practice as story writers at the Writing station.

Kindergarten

- Young children love to make stuff! Provide colored paper stapled into books for them to write their stories in. Use blank paper or paper with a picture box and a line or two at the bottom. Add a date stamp. Model how to stamp their cover with the date each time they add to or continue to work on their story. It's amazing how this simple step will keep children working on a story for more than a day.

- Kindergarteners may revise by adding details to their drawings. Model this during Writing Workshop. Post samples of revised drawings at the Writing station to remind them to revise.

- Little kids' stories often start with drawings. As they draw, prompt them to tell you their story. Ask questions that invite them to add more: *What happened next? Who else was with you? Where were you? Tell me more. Can you add some writing?*

- Acknowledge and accept the stage of writing your students are in. See the Early Developmental Writing Stages chart in the online companion, **resources.corwin.com/simplystations-writing**. Share this with parents, too, and help them understand what their children can do as writers.

Kindergartner uses a date stamp on the cover of a little book to show she is working on it across multiple days.

Grades 1–2

- Remember that story writing begins with *telling* stories, even in first and second grade.

- Students in first and second grade enjoy making books with stories, too. They like using colored paper—light green for beginnings, yellow for middles, and pink for endings. Provide paper with more lines and smaller picture boxes than kids used in kindergarten. Children might add pages to include more events, especially in the middle. See printables in the online companion.

- Writers in the early grades will enjoy writing stories with stickers. You might provide stickers of animals, people, cartoon characters, or places and things they know. Limit the number of stickers they use (two or three), so the focus is on the story, not the stickers! Model how to use stickers to write a story before placing these at the Writing station.

- Finger puppets (or stick puppets) can be fun prompts for writing stories, too. Use familiar characters for students to use to tell stories with a beginning, middle, and end. They might record their story using a device and then write the words.

Magazine photo inspires a story.

Acting out a story with puppets and then writing it.

Grades 3–4

- Older students can write longer, more developed stories than they did in primary grades. Help them storyboard before writing so they are focused and don't mix up or leave out events. A blank storyboard for planning can be found in the online companion.

- Writers in these grade levels might use colored sticky notes to plan their stories on a story plot map. They could use light green for beginning, yellow for the middle, and pink for the end (like in lower grades). Provide extra yellow sticky notes. This will help them sequence events in their stories and add details once they have the basic story written on paper.

- Provide notebook paper for story writing in upper grades. You might have students write on every other line to leave room for revision.

- Students in these grade levels may enjoy writing chapter books. Big kids like to staple notebook paper together to make books. These stories may have longer, more detailed plots and more developed characters. Some kids will even write a chapter book series. The more they work with their characters, the more developed these may become.

- You might have third and fourth graders who like to write comics or graphic novels. These are forms of storytelling and may be easier for some students to write than text in paragraphs. See the online companion for a printable form for comics. Many are available on other websites, too.

- Help students in these grades examine dialogue in the stories they read. As they learn about adding conversation in stories, they often overdo it. Show them how and where dialogue adds to a story. Model how to add dialogue to your writing and to theirs.

- Older kids may learn to write brief character sketches before creating stories. Model this before expecting students to do so. A sample is included below. A character sketch is a quick depiction of what this person is like. It's easiest to answer questions about the character: What does the character look like? How old are they? What kind of personality does the character have? Where is this character and what are they doing there? This will help students relate the character to setting and set up for the kind of conflict this character might encounter and how they would respond.

Storyboarding a story before writing it.

Character sketch written with the class helps students add descriptive details when writing a story because they understand the character well before writing.

Character Sketch

Name: Jimbo

Age: 10

Personality: adventurous, does silly stuff, shows off sometimes, likes to make people laugh, kind-hearted

Where He Is: climbing a tree

What He's Doing There: seeing how high he can go

One warm spring day Jimbo and his best friend, Marcus, decided to go to the park. They were delighted to feel the warm sun. It had been a long, cold winter!

"Hey, Marcus!" yelled Jimbo. "But I can climb higher than you!"

Before Marcus could turn around, his friend had already shimmied partway up a tall, tall tree.

4. Reflect With Students

After your students have worked with this timeless standard at the Writing station, reflect on what they've done here. Be sure to include a five- to ten-minute Reflection Time after stations where children can tell others about the story writing they did at this station. You might also refer to Section 4 in this book and the online companion to jot down your ideas about the work you and your children did with writing stories. (All printables are available for free download at **resources.corwin.com/simplystations-writing**.)

Here are a few questions you might have students use to discuss what they did as writers at the Writing station. (Use these during cleanup time with older readers.) During Reflection Time, you can ask these questions again to learn more about what students did at this station today. There are matching printables in the online companion that you can place at the Writing station if you work with intermediate students.

1. How did you start your story? Tell two events from your story in order.

2. Read a descriptive detail you wrote about a character in your story.

3. What did you revise or change in your story today? Why?

Timeless Writing Standard 3

The student will write and organize informational texts about topics of interest with text features and structures.

Let's take a closer look at this timeless standard before we begin teaching and moving it into a Writing station. Look closely at your own state standards for specific grade-level expectations and academic vocabulary. By teaching this standard well, children will be able to apply what they've learned about text features and structures in reading as they *write* informational texts. After they learn about writing informational text, add this as an option to the Writing station along with anchor charts and other supports to help students add labels, captions, and graphics to their pieces as they write about things they are interested in. They will also be able to organize their writing using informational text structures, such as description, chronological order, or compare and contrast.

What It Is

- Informational text is a type of nonfiction.

- Informational text includes the following:

  ○ Informative/explanatory: Texts that give information about the natural or social world (books, articles, field guides)

  ○ Persuasive: Texts that influence a reader's ideas or behaviors (letters, brochures, advertisements, editorials)

  ○ Nonfiction narrative: Tell stories of real events and include research in a story-like format (historical pieces, fact-based stories)

  ○ Biography: Tell about the lives of real people (memoirs, autobiographies)

  ○ Procedural: Texts that tell how to do something (how-to books, recipes)

- When writing informational text, authors include text features, such as headings, labels, captions, tables of contents, indexes, and charts, to give readers information that is clear and comprehendible.

- Authors of informational text use a variety of text structures to organize information for a specific purpose: description, chronological order, compare and contrast, problem and solution, and cause and effect. They use a combination of these within text, even within a paragraph!

Why It's Important

- Reading and writing informational text helps students learn about the world around them. It taps into their natural sense of wonder and curiosity.

- Informational text answers questions children have about why and how things work. As they read and write about topics of interest, their questions and understanding deepen.

- Not all students like to write made-up stories. Some prefer writing information about topics of interest to them.

- Writing informational text helps students develop specialized vocabulary as they learn terms that relate to particular topics, especially in content areas (e.g., *magnet, gravity, poles, conduct*).

- Writing in social studies, science, and math can extend learning in these areas as children synthesize what they've learned in pictures and words.

- Applying what they've learned about text features and structures in reading will add depth to students' informational text writing.

Myths and Confusions

- Writing a report about an animal is informational text writing. But there's so much more kids can do! They can write about topics of interest beyond animals and plants. I have met kids who are fascinated by the ocean, magnets, electricity, rocks, license plates, teeth, rainbows, or the military. Have them write about what they know and have experience with.

- Informational text writing doesn't have to be just report writing. Students can write information books, brochures, infographics, directions, field guides, observation logs, and advertisements, to name a few.

- Instead of insisting that all students write about the same topic, teach them how to discover their own passions and interests. Model writing about something your students know and connect to, and give them a choice of writing about what they know (or are interested in).

- Don't focus on too much in a lesson about informational text writing. Show kids how to make one or two writing moves at a time. For example, focus on using a few text features. When students can effectively incorporate these, move to teaching them how to use one or two text structures.

- Let children write multiple pieces about the same topic if they choose to. The more they write about a topic they're passionate about, the more they'll learn.

- Don't give kids pages where they just fill in a blank to write information. Teach with high-quality picture books and articles, so they can learn how authors craft a variety of informational text. Use the ideas on model text selection in the Plan segment that follows.

- While the emphasis on informational text writing in schools is often done on paper, students also need to learn to craft and compose multi-modal and digital text.

Real-World Connections

- Informational text surrounds us. Help students be on the lookout for information in their everyday lives—news articles, signs, YouTube videos, advertisements, email, text messages, brochures, recipes, experiments, directions.

- Most adults write informational text daily but rarely write stories. We make lists, send emails and texts, and post on social media.

- Learning to communicate information in writing will enable our students to share with others on paper and online. Today, increasing amounts of information are being shared digitally by blogging, sending emails and texts, and creating social media posts.

- Writing to share information is critical at school, in the workplace, and in society. Clear communication can prevent problems, increase productivity, and improve understanding.

How Practice at the Writing Station Helps Students

- As students write informational text with a partner at this station, they have a built-in accountability partner to listen and give feedback on what they are writing.

- Thinking and talking about what they are writing can help children clarify information they want to share with others.

- By applying to their writing what they have learned about informational text features and structures, students will become more aware of these in the informational texts they read. This can improve reading comprehension and strengthen reading-writing connections.

- Organizing information with a partner helps kids think more deeply about how to communicate what they are learning with others.

It's important to teach concepts well in whole group before moving this work into the Writing station. This will help students to eventually know how to practice the same activities with another child independently of you. Consider the following steps for whole group instruction to ensure student success with this standard.

1. Plan

Select Informational Picture Books, Articles, and Online Text

Think carefully about the kinds of informational text you use for modeling in read-aloud and shared reading, because these will be examples for the writing you expect your students to do.

Start by looking for informational text that has topics your students can easily connect to. Choose subjects from their everyday lives. Over time and across the grade levels, move away from students' known worlds to new topics they have less experience with but that will expand their learning.

Find text that is close in length and complexity to what you expect them to compose. Search for informational text with features you want your students to use in their writing. Be realistic and build their text feature repertoire slowly and carefully. A little goes a long way! Ditto for text structures.

See the chart on the next page for specifics related to finding informational texts to model with at your grade level. (See Section 4 for some sample titles, too.)

TIME-SAVING TIP: Look for text that matches topics children will be learning about in social studies and science to maximize class time.

KINDERGARTEN	GRADES 1–2	GRADES 3–4
• Short informational texts with just one to two lines per page	• Informational text with two to four lines per page for first grade	• Informational text with two to three longer paragraphs per page
• Strong picture-to-text match	• Informational text with one to two short paragraphs per page for second grade	• Graphics to match text on every double-page spread
• One or two simple text features used (e.g., title, labels, photos or graphics)	• Strong picture to text match	• More text features used in one text
• Topics related to children's experiences at home or school (pets, going to the store or the park, water, food, plants, farm or zoo animals, weather)	• Two or three simple text features used (e.g., headings, bold words, glossary, labels, captions, timeline) for first grade	• Expanded text features (e.g., sections, tables, graphs, bullets, numbers, italicized fonts)
• Simple text structures (description, chronological order, question and answer)	• More complex text features used (e.g., maps, diagrams, table of contents, index) for second grade	• Text boxes include expanded information
• New vocabulary in bold or used as one-word labels	• May include more than one simple text structure (description, chronological order, question and answer) in the text	• Expanded content area vocabulary included
	• Compare and contrast or cause and effect text structure may be used (by end of first grade)	• Wider range of text structures (may be more than one used within a paragraph)

Think Ahead About Topics, Text Features and Structures, and Writing Forms for Modeling

Just as thinking about characters and setting ahead of time is important when writing a story, thinking about your topic before modeling writing will save time when writing informational text in front of your students. Have a graphic organizer handy, too, to jot down notes about your topic as you plan your writing.

You might bookmark photos on your device ahead of time, so that you can think aloud about these with your class as you select graphics for your informational text. Plan which text features and structures to show in your model text and when you write aloud in front of your kids.

Decide ahead of time what form your informational writing might take (e.g., book, article, brochure, procedural text, field guide). Think about expanding your students' genre repertoire for informational text writing as you do so.

2. Teach

Model in Whole Group Write Aloud

During writing time it's important to show kids *how* to write an informational text. Refer to your model text frequently as you think aloud about what an author does to share information. You might use a simple graphic organizer or sticky notes and jot down a few facts you plan to include. Be explicit as you think aloud about the information you will include and why. Do this for the words you write, the photos or illustrations you choose, and the limited text features you use. Talk about why you use each of these. See the model lessons in this section for ideas.

Use a Simple Thinking Map or Sticky Notes to Plan the Information You'll Include

I like to use a circle map to jot down a few ideas I'll include in my writing, especially when working with Grades K–1. Don't write too much on these, or kids may try writing their whole piece on the thinking map and end up frustrated. Tell your class this is a place to organize your ideas before writing them.

For older students, you might use a tree map and more expanded notes before writing to organize what you want to include. Or you might model how to take notes on small sticky notes and then organize these before writing. See the online companion for printables of these maps.

Circle map filled out before modeling writing in first grade. Later this is placed at the Writing station for support.

Name __Mrs. Diller__

Las nubes estaban en el
cielo. Las pajaros volaban.
¡Aquí viene un tornado!

Modeled writing of a page using information from the circle map.

Reuse Anchor Charts From Reading to Make Connections to Writing

Refer to anchor charts you made with the class when teaching students how to use text features and structures as readers. This time, remind kids what to do as writers of informational text. If you want kindergartners to use labels matching their informational drawings, model how to do this while pointing to the text feature anchor chart you made as a class during reading instruction. Likewise, if your third graders are learning to organize information that is chronological, refer to the reading anchor chart on that text structure while modeling how to write in front of them. (You'll find anchor chart examples and related lessons for informational text features and structures in *Simply Stations: Partner Reading*.)

Anchor charts used at the Partner Reading station will be used to teach writing informational text and later placed at the Writing station. Kindergarten text features on the left; third-grade compare and contrast text structure is shown on the right.

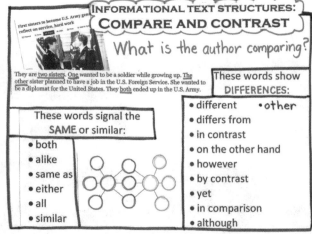

Begin With a Strong Lead and End With Concluding Sentences When Writing Information

Read informational text like a writer. Show kids how to pay attention to the way authors begin their pieces. Some use a question, others simply name the topic, still others lead with a strong fact that the reader will connect to. Create a chart of strong leads for informational text. Add examples over time as the class reads new books and articles together. Remind kids to use this when they start their pieces.

Do the same with endings of informational text. Some end with a call to action, while others end with questions or a section titled "For More Information." Make another chart of ways to conclude your informational text. Add to this periodically. Invite students to also add sticky notes to these charts of good leads and endings they found while they read independently.

Make a chart with students showing the parts of a short informational text, including a strong lead, concluding sentences, and organized information in between. Help kids think about their own writing following this pattern.

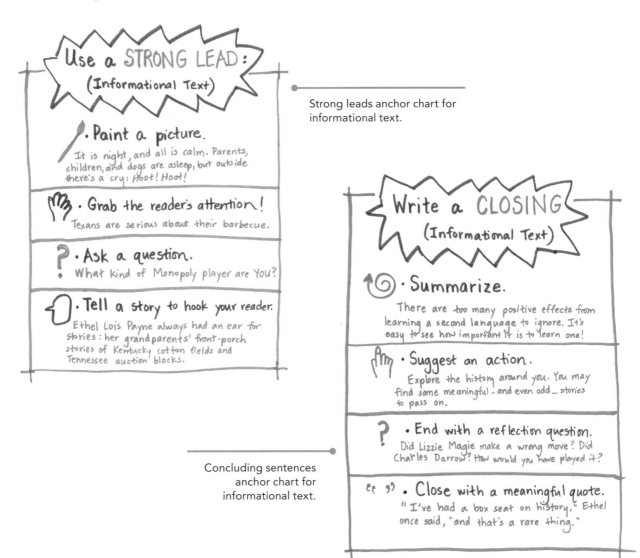

Strong leads anchor chart for informational text.

Concluding sentences anchor chart for informational text.

Use Conversation Cards to Develop Academic Vocabulary

To help children use academic vocabulary as they talk about their writing, model with conversation cards in whole group. You can use these cards or adjust them slightly to reflect the exact academic vocabulary your state uses. Post conversation cards on the board in your whole group area and have kids use them when speaking about their informational text writing. Then move them to the Writing station for students to use as they talk with each other about their writing. There are printable conversation cards in the online companion that match the lessons that follow.

The next several pages contain two sample lessons for modeling that you can use when teaching children about writing informational text during whole group instruction. One lesson is for Grades K–1 students learning how to incorporate simple text features as they write informational books about a topic of their choice. The other lesson is for intermediate learners and shows how to think about text structure as they organize information while writing. Please use these as examples to get you started with strong whole group lessons that will then be transferred to partner practice at the Writing station.

Read aloud books during your reading block that will become model texts to use again as children learn to write informational text (but not necessarily the same day). Teach these lessons more than once and watch children become more proficient at writing their own pieces with text features and structures. Substitute different text as you teach the lessons multiple times. Write aloud more than one of your own pieces with your class. Use topics your students will connect to. Model, model, model!

SAMPLE WRITING LESSON WITH A MODEL TEXT in PRIMARY GRADES

MODEL TEXT: *Hey, Water!* by Antoinette Portis (simple informational text with labels and just one to two lines of text per page)

TIMELESS STANDARD: The student will write and organize informational texts about topics of interest using text features. (The focus in this lesson is text *features*. Teach text structures in other lessons. Be sure this reflects your state and grade-level standards; adjust accordingly.)

TEACHER TALK:

- Writers choose a topic when they write. All their pictures and words go with that topic.

- Organize information about your topic. Put parts about the same thing together.

- Use text features like a title, labels, and graphics (pictures) to tell important information.

STUDENT TALK: Use the conversation cards to demonstrate. These printables are available in the online companion, **resources.corwin .com/simplystations-writing**. Kids will use these in whole group and at the Writing station, too.

- My **topic** is _____.

- I used the **text feature**, _____, to _____.

LESSON STEPS:

The goal is for students eventually to use text features well enough that they can continue to do this without teacher assistance when writing an informational text at the Writing station. The following lesson might be taught over several days. Observe your students, and have them do just a bit at a time with success so they'll want to keep writing!

1. Read the model text to your class during read-aloud prior to using it during writing time.

2. Show the book cover and tell kids you're going to use this book to think about how authors use text features to give information when writing. Ask them to pretend they are the author of the model text. Read the title and ask what the topic is (e.g., *My topic is water.*).

3. Display and quickly review a text features anchor chart you made with the class previously during reading instruction.

4. Say, *Let's pretend we are the author of this book. We used text features to give information. Name a text feature from the cover. You can use the chart. What information does the text feature give readers?* Get kids to tell information from text features used (e.g., *I used the text feature, **title**, to tell this book is about water. The text feature, **picture**, shows waves which are water. The text feature, **graphic** of a girl, shows you can swim in water. You wear goggles and a swimsuit when you swim.*).

5. Show students a page from the book and have them continue to name a text feature the author used and what readers learn from it (e.g., *I used a **label**, faucet. It goes with the **graphic**. We turn the faucet to fill a glass with water.*). Do this with a few pages.

6. Tell kids they can make an informational book, too. Before class, choose a topic your students know something about (e.g., playground, clouds, coins) and make a circle map with the topic on the inside. Show them your map and write three or four words that go with your topic that might be labels in your book. See the sample below.

7. Have students turn and talk for a minute about a topic they know about. Then give each a circle map and have them write their topic in the middle and words in the outer circle that might be a label to match their topic. Let them use pictures and words to communicate.

8. The next day, review how authors use text features to give information. Show how to use your circle map to write one or two pages for your book. Think aloud as you write a few words on a page and add a label and graphic to match. Think aloud about the information you want readers to understand from your text features.

9. Give kids paper to start making their own books in a similar way. As they write independently, circulate among them, and encourage them to add labels and matching graphics to go with their topic.

10. Be sure to take a few minutes after independent writing for several students to share their writing. Have others name text features they noticed and information they learned from the text feature. Continue in this way for multiple days, allowing students to complete books and start new ones on topics they choose.

Teacher-made circle map showing a familiar topic and possible label words on left. Modeled writing using a circle map to the right.

QUICK ASSESS:

Did students use and identify text features in books they read and wrote? Did their writing stay focused on one topic throughout a book? Did they use labels and matching graphics to give information?

AUTHOR'S CRAFT CONNECTION:

Use author's craft cards to help students notice the technique the author used to make labels look different from the rest of the text. Authors use a variety of styles to create labels. In the model text, the author used stamps to write the labels on the page. In other books, some authors use bold print or a different font for labels. At the Writing station, provide sample texts for children to use as reference where authors created labels using different techniques. The goal is for students to understand this concept well enough that they can find and make labels in their own informational text writing without teacher assistance at the Writing station. A printable card for kids to use at the station is found in the online companion, **resources.corwin.com/simplystations-writing**.

- Find labels in this informational book.

- What does the label tell?

- How does the label look different from the other words?

Model text, *Hey, Water!*, uses labels; a page a kindergartner made by stamping a label.

READING CONNECTION:

Continue to help students find and pay attention to text features as they read informational text. They will enjoy pretending they are the author. Invite them to use the conversation cards from this lesson to talk about how the author used text features to give readers information.

MOVING THIS LESSON TO PARTNER PRACTICE AT A STATION:

At the Writing station, add the option of "I can write an informational text with text features" to the display there. Include the same conversation cards, anchor charts, and writing samples from the lesson for kids to use there, but only after they show understanding of how to do this. They may need several models!

Writing station with I Can option and samples of informational text displayed.

SAMPLE WRITING LESSON WITH A MODEL TEXT in INTERMEDIATE GRADES

MODEL TEXT: "Three Notable African-American Inventors of the 18th Century" by National Geographic Society, adapted by Newsela staff https://newsela.com/read/natgeo-elem-african-american-inventors/id/44816 (informational text related to your science or social studies content with two or three text structures)

TIMELESS STANDARD: The student will write and organize informational texts about topics of interest using text *structures*. (The focus in this lesson is text *structures*. Teach text features in other lessons. Be sure this reflects your state and grade-level standards; adjust accordingly.)

TEACHER TALK:

- Writers organize information when they write. They put like ideas together.

- Authors use a variety of text structures to organize their ideas.

- Writers might **describe** a person, an animal, or an event. Then they may **compare and contrast** it to something else. They may use **chronological** order if writing about life cycles or how things are made. They may write about **problems** related to their topic and possible **solutions** or **causes** and **effects**.

- Think about the information you want your reader to know and understand. Then organize it in a way that helps the reader understand the information and your purpose for writing.

STUDENT TALK: Use conversation cards to model the talk that's expected. Have students choose the ones that match their writing. Use printables found in the online companion, **resources.corwin.com/simplystations-writing**; kids will use these at the Writing station, too.

- My **topic** is _____, and all the information I've included goes with it.

- In this part I'm **describing** _____.

- Here I'm writing about the **problem** _____ and the **solution** _____.

- In this section I'm **comparing** _____ and _____. I used the words _____ to show this.

- I **organized** this writing in **chronological order** because _____.

- Here I've included the **cause**, _____, and the **effect**, _____.

- I used the **text structure**, _____, here to _____.

LESSON STEPS:

The goal is for students to eventually use text structures to organize their writing well enough that they can continue to practice this without teacher assistance at the Writing station.

1. During reading time, read the model text and think aloud about the author's use of text structures. Place yellow sticky notes in the text labeling the text structures found. (In this particular Newsela article, you'll find description, cause and effect, and chronological order.) Use an anchor chart that lists key words that signal text structures in informational text. (See the example on the next page.)

2. During content area time, model how to take notes on a topic of study using blue sticky notes. Model how to narrow your topic. For example, instead of taking notes on Benjamin Banneker's whole life, tell students you'll read to find out about his early life and how it influenced his contributions to the world. Read from a variety texts on this topic over several days, so students learn to use more than one source for information. Model how to jot notes on blue sticky notes with one fact on each. Use the children's words, encouraging them to not just copy the text directly. Ask students if they think you have enough information to write about Banneker's early life. If not, keep finding additional sources to add information.

3. During writing time, model how to organize the sticky notes to write an informational text. Put like information together. For example, group sticky notes together that tell about Banneker's life on the farm. Place sticky notes about how he learned from his grandma in another group. You might organize these notes on an enlarged tree map. (A printable is available in the online companion and pictured on page 110.)

4. Show how to label your organized groups of blue sticky notes with yellow sticky notes that name text structures you might use. Think aloud about which you will use and why. Again, refer to the model text and key word anchor chart (e.g., _I'm going to write about Benjamin Banneker, but it will be different from the model text. It told about three inventors. I'm writing only about one of them and only about his early life._

These notes tell about the farm where he lived, so I think I'll use **description** *as my text structure to help my reader picture what Benjamin's life was like. These tell about his family and what he learned from them, so I might use* **cause and effect***.*).

5. The next day, compose one or two sentences to start an informational text in front of your class using a few of your organized blue sticky notes with yellow sticky note labels. Continue to think aloud about text structure and how you'll choose key words as you write. Use the conversation cards and refer to the anchor chart on key words that signal text structures.

6. Invite students to work in pairs to continue to write this informational piece using the organized sticky notes and labels you developed as a class. Have partners share a piece of paper and write together, referring to the resources you've been modeling with. As they write, circulate around the classroom, talking with pairs about how they're organizing their ideas and what text structures they're using and why. Encourage them to use the conversation cards as they talk about their writing. Ask several kids to share at the end of writing time while the rest of the class gives them feedback.

7. Continue this process of writing and organizing informational text over time. Have students work alone or in pairs to read and take notes about topics of interest. (See *Simply Stations: Listening and Speaking* for additional ideas on note-taking.) Then have them organize their notes using a tree map and think about which text structures to use as they write informational pieces.

Model text with yellow sticky notes labeling text structures.

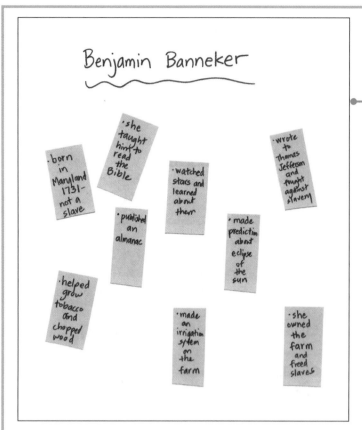

Teacher notes on the topic of study, Benjamin Banneker, using blue sticky notes.

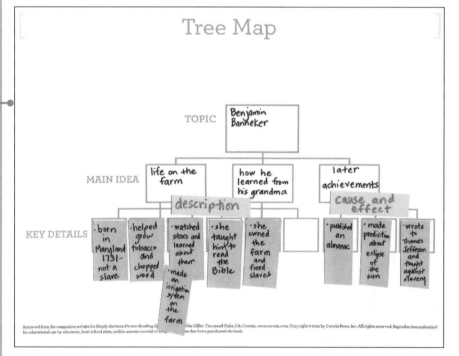

Blue sticky notes organized into groups with text structure yellow sticky note labels added.

QUICK ASSESS:

Could students identify the text structures used by an author and tell why? Were they able to help organize blue sticky notes into groups that made sense? Did they use text structures to organize their information when writing and could they tell why?

AUTHOR'S CRAFT CONNECTION:

Use author's craft cards to help students think about how writers use headings to organize information into sections. Have them use the cards as they talk about informational books and articles as well as their own writing and that of their peers. The goal is for students to understand this well enough that they can add headings to organize their writing at the Writing station without teacher assistance. A printable card for kids to use at the station is found in the online companion.

- Look at how the author organized the writing into sections. What is this section about? How do you know?

- Find a heading. How does it look different from the rest of the text? Why did the author use this heading?

READING CONNECTION:

As you teach students to write informational text using text structures, be sure to remind them to look for these in the reading they're doing, too. Understanding how and why authors use text structures to organize their reading will deepen students' reading comprehension.

MOVING THIS LESSON TO PARTNER PRACTICE AT A STATION:

At the Writing station, add the option of "I can organize my informational text writing using text structures." Include the same conversation cards, anchor charts, and writing samples from this lesson for kids to use at the Writing station, but only after they show understanding of how to do this. It will take more than one lesson! Encourage partners to use the conversation cards to talk with each other about their writing here.

3. Partner Practice

Once you see students are able to understand and use text features and structures during writing time, you're ready to move that same work into partner practice at the Writing station.

At first, some students may copy what they saw you do while writing informational text. But over time, they will take risks to try new things as they experience success and gain confidence. Here are some additional, grade-specific suggestions to help you think about the best things for your children to practice.

Kindergarten

- Display an ongoing list of topics kindergartners may want to write about at your Writing station. Add to it as you study new things in science or social studies (e.g., weather, magnets, rocks, recycling, citizenship, flags, maps, globes). Include a photo or sketch beside each. Include things they know from day-to-day life, too (e.g., teeth, hair, shoes, pencils, riding the bus, pets, celebrations).

- Kindergarten children love to make stuff! Model how to make little books by stapling pages together. They might make informational books, field guides, guidebooks about your school or familiar places, or how-to books. You might also show how to make simple brochures by folding paper in half. After modeling well during writing time, place these same materials and a sample or two at the Writing station.

- Likewise, model how to make field guides with drawings or photos of familiar birds and animals. You might place binoculars near a window with clipboards and pencils for kids to use to sketch birds or provide a digital camera to take photos of them. Include a child-friendly field guide or two there, too. Name this the "Field Guide station" for fun!

Chart of informational text writing topics for young writers to display at the Writing station.

Field Guide station materials.

Grades 1–2

- First and second graders enjoy making things, too. Provide modeling and materials using ideas from the kindergarten list. But model at a slightly higher level matching your students' skills and learning goals.

- Model how to make question and answer books. In first grade, write a question on the left-hand page and the answer on the page to the right. In second grade, you might write the question at the top and the answer at the bottom and even onto the next page. Kids will enjoy making these at the Writing station, too. You might do the same with problem-and-solution books or cause-and-effect books to help younger readers understand these text structures.

- Students in these grade levels enjoy informational text series, such as Who Would Win? by Jerry Pallotta. After reading and thinking aloud about how the author organized information, kids might like making their own Who Would Win? books at the Writing station.

- By the end of first grade, students may enjoy reading and writing simple biographies or even autobiographies. This is a great genre for them to examine text structures, such as chronological order and description. Biography can become another option of what to write at the Writing station over time.

- Procedural or how-to text is another informational genre for you to explore with your students. Teach students about text features and structures used in this genre before moving kids into writing procedural text. You might start by doing shared writing of directions for things your class does at school. Over time, kids might write how-to text at the Writing station.

First grader discovers he loves to write when he creates his own Who Would Win? book.

- In upper elementary grades, kids still like making things. Let them make informational books with extended text features and structures. Later in the year, add brochures or procedural directions or biographies. Add options to your I Can list with samples as you introduce new possibilities of what children can make at the Writing station. Be sure to model these types of writing before moving them into this station.

- Post anchor charts of expanded text features and text structures at the Writing station after kids have been taught how to incorporate these into their writing.

- Incorporate digital texts into teaching kids about writing informational text. You might teach upper-grade students how to make infographics related to topics they're studying about in content areas. Again, post samples labeled with what to include. They can use Canva or Google Drawings to create their own. Likewise, for multimodal texts, teach kids how to create multimedia posters, YouTube videos, or slideshows in Google Slides, PowerPoint or Prezi, by first writing out an organizational plan for the information they'll present.

- Encourage older kids to include specialized vocabulary in their informational text writing. Model with your own writing to show them how to use bold words and a glossary defining those terms.

- Display writing expectations on a board by your Writing station to help students focus on what to do as writers. It might read:

  Did you include . . .

  ○ A strong lead?

  ○ Concluding sentences?

  ○ Text features that support information?

  ○ Text structures that organize your ideas?

4. Reflect With Students

After your students have worked with this timeless standard at the Writing station, reflect on what they've done here. Be sure to include a five- to ten-minute Reflection Time after stations and small group where children can tell others what they've learned. The online companion contains printable templates where you can jot down your ideas about the work you and your students did.

Children may use the questions below during cleanup time to talk about the work that they did at the Writing station. During Reflection Time, you can ask these questions again to learn more about what students did at this station today. (There are matching printables in the online companion that you can place at the Writing station. Visit **resources.corwin.com/simplystations-writing** for these resources and more.)

1. Which topic did you write an informational text about today? Did all your words and graphics go with your topic? Show an example.

2. Did you add any text features to your writing? Show a text feature you used and tell why.

3. How did you organize your information when writing? What text structure did you use? Share an example.

Timeless Writing Standard 4

The student will write to express an opinion about a topic with reasons for support.

Let's take a look at this timeless standard before we begin teaching and moving it into a Writing station. Review closely your own state standards for grade-level expectations and academic vocabulary.

Kindergartners will usually learn how to tell and then write their opinions about books heard or read. They might also share opinions about topics they have experience with. In first and second grade, students are expected to write opinions about texts and topics. By third and fourth grade, they learn to write persuasive pieces. After learning to express opinions and using these to persuade others, pairs of students may practice doing these same tasks alone or with a partner at the Writing station.

What It Is

- An opinion is what you think or feel about something or someone. It's a strong belief that a person has formed about a topic.

- People can have different opinions they express by speaking or by writing.

- You may agree or disagree with someone else's opinion.

- Feelings and experiences help to shape people's opinions.

- An opinion is stronger when based on facts and should be stated with reasons for support.

- Giving reasons for one's opinions strengthens arguments that can be used to persuade others to change behaviors.

Why It's Important

- Being able to state opinions helps students become self-confident as they articulate what they think or believe.

- Telling opinions with personal reasons to support them helps speakers and writers develop voice.

- Supporting opinions with facts helps speakers and writers develop credibility.

- Writing opinions helps kids understand how opinions differ from facts. And the ability to differentiate between fact and opinion improves students' critical thinking skills.

Myths and Confusions

- Kids often have trouble telling the difference between facts and opinions. Start with topics they know and have experience with when teaching them the difference. Have them sort facts from opinions (e.g., *Washington Elementary is the name of our school* vs. *school is fun*).

- There's a difference between preferences and opinions. Preferences are choosing one thing over another (e.g., *I like the color blue better than yellow*). Opinions have more to do with beliefs and feelings. Opinions are stronger and are based on experiences (e.g., *My bedroom should be painted blue because it's my favorite color and blue calms me*).

- Young children develop preferences early, especially around food. They may refuse to eat certain things (even though they never tasted them), because they have developed opinions about these foods. Eventually, preferences may grow into opinions. For example, my granddaughter had the opinion that strawberries were yucky until she finally tasted them. Then her opinion was, "Strawberries are delicious, and everyone should try them!"

- Help students write opinion pieces about things they have experience with and strong feelings about. Don't have them write about random topics pulled from a hat.

- Writing an opinion should be more than just "I like" or "I don't like." Help students learn to use more advanced vocabulary as they express their opinions and give specific reasons for them. See the chart, Words to Use When Expressing Opinions, on page 127 for specifics.

Real-World Connections

- Opinions greatly shape personal behavior. Again, think about food. What we prefer to eat helps us determine what we buy at the grocery store and which restaurants we frequent.

- Stating one's opinion strongly and with well-thought out reasons often influences the behavior of others. For example, opinions are widely prevalent in politics.

- Everyday news media and advertisers share opinions and facts. Knowing the difference can make us wiser consumers of information and adept critical thinkers.

- Social media influencers share their opinions about products online and affect people's purchases. Again, knowing the difference between opinion and fact can make us better consumers.

- Opinions can be stated in a variety of forms in the world: signs, editorials, book reviews, persuasive letters, speeches, dinner discussions.

How Practice at the Writing Station Helps Students

- Talking with a partner about an opinion at the Writing station can strengthen children's writing of opinion pieces there. As they share by speaking first, they can better formulate ideas to then put in writing.

- As students write opinions at this station, they have a built-in accountability partner to listen and give feedback on what they are writing.

- Thinking and talking about what they are writing can help children strengthen their reasons and examples to share with others.

- By writing opinions at the Writing station, children will have a deeper understanding of opinions when they read as well. This can improve reading comprehension and help them develop critical thinking.

Students must understand what an opinion is before they can write their own with conviction. Spend ample time having children talk about opinions before they move into writing them. Be sure they talk and write about things for which they have strong feelings and experiences! You will want to explicitly model how to craft opinion pieces, teaching kids to include an opening or introduction, reasons and examples, and a closing or conclusion. Do this multiple times until you observe that students are ready to do this with a partner as an option at the Writing station.

Consider the following steps for whole group instruction to ensure student success with this standard.

1. Plan

Select Opinion Pieces for Model Texts

Because you'll be modeling the work students will eventually do in the Writing station, think about this standard and the kinds of experiences and texts that will help kids successfully express opinions both verbally and in writing.

I recommend four kinds of text to look for when teaching students about opinion writing. Each has a different purpose. See the charts that follow for examples of each.

TIME-SAVING TIP:
When looking online for nonfiction articles with opinions in children's news magazines, search for the words *should, important, good,* or *best* in the titles. Or, do a search for *opinion* or *debate* on the site.

1. You might first read aloud a few **fiction books** to help kids understand what an opinion is. I've listed stories below where authors included characters with opinions who were trying to persuade someone to think or do something. These are *not* examples of the kind of writing you will expect your students to do, but can help kids understand what opinions are. Have students identify characters' opinions and give reasons for them based on text evidence.

2. Read aloud **nonfiction books** teaching kids about how to write opinions. This genre has been growing lately as teachers are teaching young students in elementary grades to write opinions. Use a lot of these! They are excellent model texts to use as examples to teach kids how to write their own opinion pieces.

3. Also share **opinion articles from magazines and news sites**. These should closely mirror the types of opinion writing you expect your students to do with support and practice. Use these as model texts mostly with older elementary kids. Adjust the reading levels to match those of your students.

4. Finally, read aloud **picture books about activists**. These narratives will share how voicing opinions can change history. They are the *why* of expressing opinions! Again, have kids identify the opinions of these activists and how they brought about change.

EL TIP: Help multilingual learners share their experiences and opinions about injustices they or their families might have experienced. Learn from and with your students.

FICTION BOOKS WITH CHARACTERS WHO EXPRESS OPINIONS

KINDERGARTEN	GRADES 1–2	GRADES 3–4
• *Don't Let the Pigeon Drive the Bus!* by Mo Willems	• *Layla's Happiness* by Mariahadessa Ekere Tallie	• *The Perfect Pet* by Margie Palatini
• *The Big Bed* by Bunmi Laditan	• *Don't Feed the Bear* by Kathleen Doherty	• *Front Desk* by Kelly Yang
• *Red Is Best* by Kathy Stinson	• *One Word from Sophia* by Jim Averbeck	• *Earrings!* by Judith Viorst
• *I Like Myself!* by Karen Beaumont	• *Can I Be Your Dog?* By Troy Cummings	• *Have I Got a Book for You!* by Mélanie Watt
	• *I Will Never Not Ever Eat a Tomato* by Lauren Child	• *Persuading Miss Doover* by Robin Pulver
	• *Facts vs. Opinions vs. Robots* by Mike Rex	• *I Wanna Iguana* by Karen Kaufman Orloff (series of I Wanna books)
	• *I Want a Dog: My Opinion Essay; I Want a Cat: My Opinion Essay* both by Darcy Pattison (each includes a sample opinion piece)	• *What Do You Think, Katie?* by Fran Manushkin

NONFICTION BOOKS ABOUT OPINION WRITING

KINDERGARTEN	GRADES 1–2	GRADES 3–4
• What's Your Point? series by Tony Stead from Capstone (five books for each grade written by kids, for kids; e.g., *What Is the Best Pet?*; *How You Can Be a Good Friend*)	• What's Your Point? series by Tony Stead (e.g., *Should We Squash Bugs?* for first grade or *Why Should We Recycle?* for second grade) • Seeing Both Sides series from Rourke (six books for Grades 1–3, e.g., *Junk Food, Yes or No*; *TV, Yes or No*) • *Pick a Picture, Write an Opinion!* by Kristen McCurry	• What's Your Point? series by Tony Stead (e.g., *Should Children Have Homework?* for third grade or *What Is the Most Important Invention?* for fourth grade) • Seeing Both Sides series from Rourke (eight books for Grades 3–6, e.g., *Class Parties, Yes or No*; *Summer School, Yes or No*) • Shape Your Opinion series from Norwood House (six books, e.g., *Should Kids Get Allowance?*; *Should Kids Use Social Media?*)

ARTICLES FOR OPINION WRITING

LOOK FOR ARTICLES THAT	GRADES 2–4
• Are short • Have a clearly stated opinion • Have reasons and strong examples to support them • Have a conclusion that restates the opinion with enthusiasm • Show both sides of an argument, if possible	Look at these news sites for articles: • www.newsela.com • www.timeforkids.com • https://sn3.scholastic.com/pages/topics/debates.html?page=1 (Scholastic News debate topics)

Picture Books About Activists

This is not a complete list, but rather just a few titles to get you started. Look for people who changed the world. Ask students what beliefs these people and others at the time held. What were people's opinions about the issues surrounding these activists?

KINDERGARTEN AND GRADE 1	GRADES 2–4
• *The Pink Hat* by Andrew Joyner • *The Story of Ruby Bridges* by Robert Coles • *Hands Up!* by Breanna J. McDaniel • *Never Too Young!: 50 Unstoppable Kids Who Made a Difference* by Aileen Weintraub	• *The Power of Her Pen* by Lesa Cline-Ransome • *She Persisted* by Chelsea Clinton • *The Little Book of Activists* by Penguin Young Readers • *You Are Mighty* by Caroline Paul (use "A Note from the Author" as a model text) • *Enough! 20 Protestors Who Changed America* by Emily Easton • *Shaking Things Up* poems by Susan Hood • *Pride: The Story of Harvey Milk and the Rainbow Flag* by Rob Sanders • *Be the Change: A Grandfather Gandhi Story* by Arun Gandhi and Bethany Hegedus • *Stories for Kids Who Dare to Be Different* by Ben Brooks • *The Youngest Marcher: The Story of Audrey Fay Hendricks, a Young Civil Rights Activist* by Cynthia Levinson • *Separate Is Never Equal: Sylvia Mendez and Her Family's Fight for Desegregation* by Duncan Tonatiuh

You might also show students short video clips on kids who are activists. Have your students listen for what this person was passionate about. What problem did they identify? (Topic and opinion emerge from this.) How did they bring about change? Search for pieces with the child activist talking at the ages listed on the next page. Here are a few suggestions.

- **Marley Dias**: A young Black girl who began a social media campaign for #1000BlackGirlBooks at age ten and wrote a book at age twelve, *Marley Dias Gets It Done: And So Can You*

- **Mari Copeny** (a.k.a. Little Miss Flint): An eight-year-old Black girl who wrote a letter to President Barack Obama about the water crisis in her city of Flint, Michigan, and began a bottled water campaign to distribute more than a million bottles of water to her community

- **Xiuhtezcatl Martinez**: A Native American male who spoke publicly at age six about saving our earth and today is a hip-hop artist and youth director of Earth Guardians, a worldwide conservation organization

- **Sophie Cruz**: A five-year-old who ran past a barricade in Washington, D.C., and shared a message with Pope Francis about her undocumented immigrant family from Oaxaca, Mexico, and continues to fight for immigrant rights today

- **Bana al-Abed**: A seven-year-old Syrian girl who sent Twitter messages (with help from her English-speaking mom) documenting the war in her city of Aleppo and calling for peace and published a memoir, *Dear World*

Think Ahead About Topics for Opinions

When modeling how to write in front of your class, it's important to plan ahead for what you might write about. Think about topics you have strong opinions and beliefs about that would also be of interest to your students. You can, of course, write about favorites (food, music, hobbies, sports teams). But don't be afraid to voice your beliefs about events that affect your school, community, or the world.

As you write, be sure to let kids know that this is *your* opinion and that others have their own opinions that may differ from yours. Show and tell students it is safe to voice their opinions in your classroom. To elicit passion and voice from your class, think about problems that they want to do something about. Here are some topics to consider, but ask your class for their ideas, too.

- Injustices (local problems in the news that affect kids and/or their families)

- Waste (food in the cafeteria, natural resources, taxpayers' money)

- Destruction of natural resources (wildfires, air and water pollution, erosion, animal and plant species)

Sample lists, made in two different grade levels to use for reference, follow on the next page.

Opinion topic lists generated with students (Grades K–1 on the left; third grade on the right).

We can write **OPINIONS** about:

- going back to school
- cafeteria food
- water conservation
- sports teams
- cell phones
- music to listen to
- books we've read
- homework
- treating people fairly

2. Teach

Clarify Differences Between Facts and Opinions

Be sure kids know what *opinion* means before delving into work with this concept. Use the teacher talk from the lessons in this section. Encourage students to use the word, *opinion*, as they respond orally and in writing, too. Help them use facts to back their opinions as they grow in understanding.

You might use photos and have students tell an opinion about things pictured. Then have them tell facts about the photo. You might jot down students' sentences on cards or sentence strips. For example, when showing a photo of a green sea turtle kids might share these opinions: *I think sea turtles should be protected. They are beautiful ocean creatures.* Or, they might tell these facts: *Some people harvest green sea turtle eggs. Sea turtles get caught in fishing nets and die.*

Then hand the cards or strips to individuals. Have them stand up and sort themselves into one group holding *opinions* and the other showing *facts*. These photos could later be placed at the Writing station where kids could sort facts from opinions before writing opinions. Eventually, teach students how to use facts to support their opinions.

TIME-SAVING TIP:
When teaching about opinions, tap into social studies and science topics being studied.

Create Anchor Charts With Your Class

Make an anchor chart about opinions *with* your class. Jot down opinion examples on sticky notes as you hear opinions during the day (e.g., when someone gives an opinion about the lunchroom food or a book read, when you read an opinion in a piece you're reading as a class, when students share opinions they heard in the news). Place the notes around the perimeter of the chart. Examples of class anchor charts are included below.

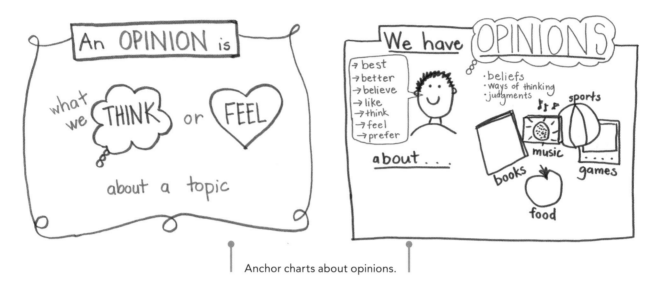

Anchor charts about opinions.

Likewise, make an anchor chart about writing opinions. Build it using a writing sample with labeled parts of this kind of text. Include labels for *opening* or *introduction, reason, example,* and *closing* or *conclusion.* Some examples follow.

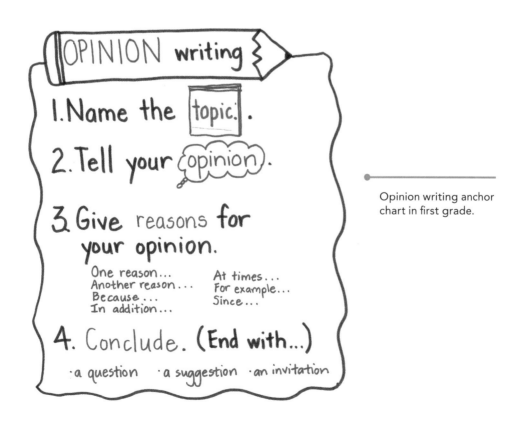

Opinion writing anchor chart in first grade.

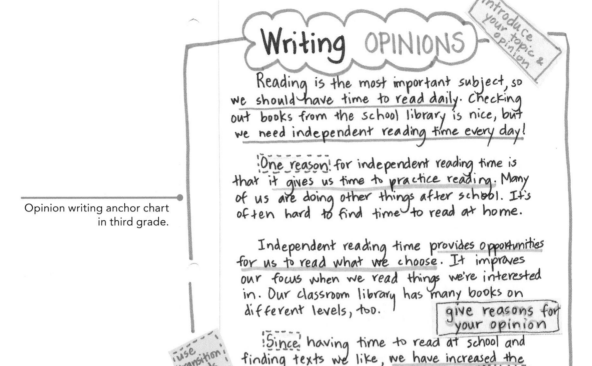

Writing OPINIONS

introduce your topic & opinion

Reading is the most important subject, so we should have time to read daily. Checking out books from the school library is nice, but we need independent reading time every day!

One reason for independent reading time is that it gives us time to practice reading. Many of us are doing other things after school. It's often hard to find time to read at home.

Independent reading time provides opportunities for us to read what we choose. It improves our focus when we read things we're interested in. Our classroom library has many books on different levels, too.

give reasons for your opinion

use transition words

Since having time to read at school and finding texts we like, we have increased the number of minutes we read each day. At first, some of us didn't even read for five minutes. Now we all read at least twenty minutes a day.

Most importantly, we are a reading community. We love to read! We choose to read! We recommend books to each other! If your class doesn't have independent reading time, you should. Tell your teacher and principal what a difference it can make.

conclude with an action

Opinion writing anchor chart in third grade.

Model How to Structure an Opinion Text

Write aloud in front of your class during writing time, so they learn *how* to write an opinion piece. Think aloud about your topic, your opinion, and why you feel this way. Model how to jot down these things along with reasons and examples first. Then use key words as you organize your thoughts, thinking aloud about the words you choose. See the chart that follows for specific words to teach students to use when writing opinions.

Words to Use When Expressing Opinions

To differentiate between opinions and other types of text, introduce your class to lists of words they might use when crafting opinions. Highlight these words as you come across them with your students in opinion texts and add them to the chart. Here is a list to help you know what to be on the lookout for, especially in Grades 2–4. A printable version is on the companion website, **resources .corwin.com/simplystations-writing**.

OPENING/ INTRODUCTORY WORDS	TRANSITION WORDS	CLOSING/ CONCLUDING WORDS
• I think	• First/second/third	• As you can see
• I believe	• Next/then/after that	• In conclusion
• My favorite	• An example	• Now you know why
• The best	• One reason	• For all the reasons
• In my opinion	• Additionally	• That's why
• I feel very strongly about	• Another	• To summarize
• I know that you will have to agree that	• In addition	• This is why
	• Besides	
	• Most importantly	

On the following pages are two lessons to use when teaching children how to write opinion texts. The first one focuses on stating an opinion in pictures and words in kindergarten and Grade 1. The other is for Grades 2–4 and has ideas for composing more sophisticated opinion pieces that include an introduction, reasons and examples, and a conclusion. Please use these whole group lessons as examples to get you started with work that can then be transferred to a choice for partner practice at the Writing station.

SAMPLE WRITING LESSON WITH A MODEL TEXT in PRIMARY GRADES

MODEL TEXT: *What Is the Best Pet?* by Tony Stead (or another book for Grades K–1 from the What's Your Point? series; if you don't have these books, show photos of several kinds of pets, such as a dog, a cat, a fish, a snake)

TIMELESS STANDARD: The student will express an opinion about a topic with reasons for support. (Be sure this reflects your state and grade-level standards.)

Supports for opinion talk for multilingual learners.

TEACHER TALK:

- People have *opinions*, or things they feel strongly about. In my opinion, **(give an example: *I think cars should go slower on my street*)**.

- People have *opinions* about a lot of things: books, foods, sports teams, or how to spend their time or money. My opinion about **(give an example: *How to spend your free time is that you shouldn't watch a lot of TV*)**.

- It's okay to tell your *opinion*, or how you feel about something. Be kind.

- Not everybody has the same *opinion*. Listen to others.

- Give *reasons* for your *opinion*. Tell why.

STUDENT TALK: Use matching printables found on the online companion. Kids will use these at the Writing station, too.

- I **think** _____ is the **best** _____.

- My **opinion** is _____. A **reason** is _____.

LESSON STEPS:

1. Talk with children about what an *opinion* is (telling how you think or feel about something). Create a simple anchor chart like the one on page 125. Discuss why it's important to tell our opinions (e.g., *It's good to have a voice and tell how you feel about something.*)

2. Show the model text after using it as a read-aloud to teach children about opinions. (See Reading Connection for ideas on using labeled colored sticky notes to teach with this book.) Ask how we can tell it's an opinion text (e.g., *best* is in the title).

3. Explain that you will write an opinion piece as a class. The topic might be why our class is the best kindergarten or first grade (something they will all agree with and feel strongly about!).

4. Refer to the model text and have children name the three things the author included (opinion, reason, end). Have them use the colored labeled sticky notes for help.

5. Have three colors of paper ready for writing—light green, yellow, and pink—that you'll staple together to make a little book. Write the class's opinion on the light green page (e.g., *We think Mr. Fenton's room is the best first grade class*). Add an illustration to match, thinking aloud about how your picture and words match. Stop here with your modeling.

6. Now have kids think about and take turns sharing aloud a topic they have an opinion about. Help them choose something they care about. Keep an ongoing list of opinion topics with illustrations to help them. (See the sample on page 124.) Have children turn and talk with a partner about their opinion. Then hand each student a green piece of paper after they tell you their opinion about their topic. Have them go to their seats to create their own first page of their opinion books.

7. The next day, review what an opinion is. Reread your writing from the day before (the green page). Then turn to the yellow page and write a reason for that opinion, such as *One reason is we bring our library books back on time.* Add another yellow page and have kids give another reason (e.g., *Our principal gives us lots of compliments*). Add words and matching pictures. Then ask kids to do the same by adding yellow pages to their opinion writing during independent writing time.

8. On the last day, repeat the process above with a pink page. Write a strong ending, such as *If you are in kindergarten, we hope you will get to be in Mr. Fenton's class next year!* Reread the book as a class and have students tell the three things they included in their class opinion piece. Then have them finish and share their opinion books.

TIME-SAVING TIP:
Don't try to keep all kids at the same place in the writing process. Let them write at their own pace, knowing some will still be stating their opinion while others have moved on to reasons. It's okay if some kids start a new piece while others are still in the middle of an old one.

Sticky notes in the model text and labeled pages in the little book the class wrote together.

QUICK ASSESS:

Can students tell the three parts of opinion writing: the opinion, the reasons, and the end? Can they express an opinion on a topic? Are they able to give two or more reasons telling why they think or feel that way? Can they end with a strong restatement of their opinion? Can they do this orally? In writing using pictures and words?

AUTHOR'S CRAFT CONNECTION:

Look at the model text and help kids notice that these opinion pieces were written by children the same age as them. Have them articulate how the pictures match the words. Discuss the details in the drawings and photos that go with the words. Use the author's craft cards found in the online companion. They will help children answer the questions that follow.

- *Find a picture. What word does it match?*

- *What details did the illustrator use in the picture? How did this tell an opinion?*

READING CONNECTION:

Prepare colored sticky notes to use with the model text (or other nonfiction opinion piece)—light green for *opinion*, yellow for *reasons*, and pink for *end*. Label them to match. Read aloud the book to your class. Then reread it and think aloud about the parts of this opinion text as you place each matching sticky note on a page. Finally, have students use opinion conversation cards and pretend they are the author to talk about the book. Have someone tell the opinion by saying, *"I think a kitten is the best pet"* or *"My opinion is that kittens are the best pet."* Then do the same with reasons: *"A reason is because they're cute and soft."* Repeat with the end (e.g., *A kitten would be a great pet!*). Point out that the author is telling his opinion again at the end in a strong way.

Reread the model text on another day and have students turn and talk to a partner, using the conversation cards to express an opinion about what they think would be the best pet. *I think _____ is the best pet. One reason is _____.* Have several students share their ideas.

MOVING THIS LESSON TO PARTNER PRACTICE AT A STATION:

At the Writing station, have kids work with a classmate to give their opinions about a topic they feel strongly about. Post a list of student-generated topics they might write their opinions about. Provide little books with colored paper to staple together, so kids can continue to write their own opinion pieces. They may write alone or with a partner here. Also place the model texts you taught with at this station as references and samples.

SAMPLE WRITING LESSON WITH A MODEL TEXT IN INTERMEDIATE GRADES

MODEL TEXT: *Stella Writes an Opinion* by Janiel Wagstaff (or use an opinion article from children's news magazines like those recommended on page 121)

TIMELESS STANDARD: The student will express an opinion about a topic with reasons for support. (Be sure this reflects your state and grade-level standards.)

TEACHER TALK:

- You can express your *opinion*, something you feel strongly about, by speaking or writing.

- You might try to *persuade* others to agree with you by sharing your *opinion*.

- Supporting your *opinion* with *reasons* and *examples* makes your *argument* stronger.

- Use *transition words* to move from one part to another when you write *opinion pieces*.

- End your *opinion text* with a *closing* or *conclusion*. Give your reader a final thought about your opinion.

STUDENT TALK: Use matching printables found on the online companion. Students will use these at the Writing station, too.

- In my **opinion**, I think that _____.
  One reason for this is _____. **Another reason** is _____.

- This is why I think that _____.

- A **transition** I used is _____.

LESSON STEPS:

1. Discuss what an opinion is. Make or refer to an anchor chart about this concept. Then read aloud part of the model text to the class each day for multiple days. Start with pages 1–11 that tell how to come up with an opinion. Then stop and make a list with students of topics they have opinions about (things they love, things they don't love, what bugs them about school and home, and what they'd change if they were in charge).

2. Have students turn and talk with a partner about some of their opinions. Then share one of your opinions. Write your topic and opinion on the printable Planning for Opinion Writing sheet found on the online companion. Ask students to do the same with one of their topics and opinions.

3. The next day, review in the model text how the main character, Stella, started with a topic and an opinion. Review Stella's opinion. Then read pages 12–18. Point out how Stella jotted down her reasons and included examples.

4. Review the opinion you wrote down yesterday and show how to list a reason for your opinion with an example on the same planning form your students are using. Then have them do the same with their own reasons and examples to match their opinions.

5. On another day, finish reading the model text. Read aloud pages 19–25. Review your opinion writing planning sheet. Jot down a sentence or two as a placeholder for your closing or conclusion. Then have kids continue to fill in their planning page.

6. Finally, model for students how to use your plan to draft your opinion piece. Think aloud as you write the introduction. Then invite them to work on their own. Continue in this way, modeling how to draft your writing over several days. Include an introduction, reasons with examples, and a closing or conclusion. You might include brief anecdotes as examples to make your writing interesting and encourage kids to do the same. Know that it's okay if all writers aren't at the same place in their writing as your demonstrations. The writing process is different for all writers! If kids finish one piece, they might start another.

TIME-SAVING TIP: When students choose their own writing topics about things they are passionate about, they will be invested in what they write and will work harder on these pieces. Don't waste time by having everyone write about the same thing.

QUICK ASSESS:

Can students identify the components of an opinion text: the topic and opinion, the reasons and examples, and the closing or conclusion? Are they able to express an opinion and give strong reasons with examples supporting why they think or feel that way? Can they conclude with a strong restatement of their opinion? Can they do this orally? In writing?

AUTHOR'S CRAFT CONNECTION:

In this model text, the author cleverly embedded how to write an opinion text into the story of Stella, a girl who must write an opinion at school. The author included some writing samples in her book, too. Use the author's craft cards found in the online companion to talk about the following:

- *How did the graphics support the opinion the author voiced?*

- *How did the author use different fonts in this text? Why?*

- *Name any text features the author used. How did these give information about an opinion?*

READING CONNECTION:

Have students read many opinion pieces before they try to write their own. Use suggestions for choosing model texts on pages 120–122. Be sure to use nonfiction books about writing opinions and opinion articles, as suggested. Have students identify components of opinion texts by underlining these in colored pencil as follows: green for topic, purple for opinion, blue for each reason, orange for examples to match the reasons, and red for the closing or conclusion. (See a sample in the following picture.) Being able to understand *how* opinion text is structured will help kids organize their thoughts when writing their own.

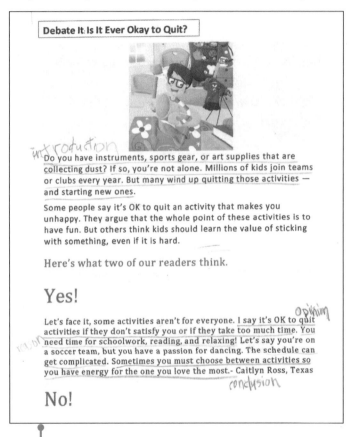

Opinion text underlined by kids with colored pencils to show components.

MOVING THIS LESSON TO PARTNER PRACTICE AT A STATION:

Partners can work together at the Writing station, sharing their opinions about topics they feel strongly about. Post a list of student-generated topics they might talk or write their opinions about. Be sure to include a model of opinion writing with components clearly labeled, as pictured on page 137. Kids may choose to write alone or with a partner here.

3. Partner Practice

Once you see that students can find topics they have opinions about and express these by talking to a partner and jotting down their opinions and reasons, they're ready to move that same work into partner practice at the Writing station. Expect learners to do what you've modeled well with those same materials and tasks in whole group lessons.

Here are some additional, grade-level specific suggestions to help you think about meaningful work your students might do at the Writing station as they focus on voicing their opinions as writers.

Kindergarten

- Focus on having students *talk* about their opinions before moving into writing them. (Practice this in whole group first!) Use opinion picture cards for partners to talk about. Have them record and then listen to their conversation. Following this, they might work together to write their opinions in pictures and words.

- Begin opinion writing by teaching kindergartners to recommend books to others, sharing personal opinions. Have them use opinion conversation cards as they share their ideas. See Timeless Standard 4 in *Simply Stations: Independent Reading* for additional suggestions.

- Model how to write opinions by including one student's opinion each day in Daily News or Morning Message. (Newspapers and magazines often include opinions, so this is a real-world application.)

- Teach kids how to make signs to voice opinions. Then add this as an option at the Writing station.

Grades 1–2

- Use ideas from kindergarten in first and second grade, too. Provide opinion topic charts and/or picture cards for students to choose topics and discuss opinions before writing. As students tell and then write book recommendations, expect them to include more details as they move up the grade levels.

- Cut up a short opinion piece into three parts: opinion, reasons, and closing. Glue each piece onto construction paper and laminate. Have kids practice putting the "puzzle" back in order. Provide colored labeled sticky notes from the model lesson for kids to label the parts and talk about each. Then have them write their own opinion pieces.

- Teach first and second graders how to write persuasive letters when expressing their opinions. This can then be added as an option at the Writing station. Display a sample written with your class to use as a reference.

- Book reviews also include opinions, so you might also add these as options for the Writing station after teaching students how to write these.

Grades 3–4

- Upper-grade students can write persuasive letters and book reviews, too, after some instruction on how to do this. At the Writing station, display samples you've written as a class.

- Newsela has pro/con articles, and Scholastic News has a debate segment. These are excellent examples of argumentative text to use with older students. Adjust the reading levels to match those of your kids. First use these in whole group or small group instruction. Then you might move one or two of them to the Writing station as examples.

- The *New York Times* contains a section called "Student Opinion." Find ones that are age appropriate for your kids and present these questions to them for discussion and response. You can find the section here: https://www.nytimes.com/column/learning-student-opinion

- Print an opinion article and cut it apart by component (introduction, reason, example, conclusion), as shown in the photo that follows. Then have kids reassemble and label it with sticky notes, talking about each part and the information it gives them. Be sure students also read the article and talk about the author's opinion and if they agree or disagree and why. This can help them review how to write opinion pieces before composing their own.

- Play "Opinion Volley" in whole or small group before moving this to the Writing station. Have partners select a topic. Then they take turns going back and forth giving opinions on it until they run out of ideas. Use this as a warm-up before writing opinions.

Fourth graders talk about and write opinions using news articles posted.

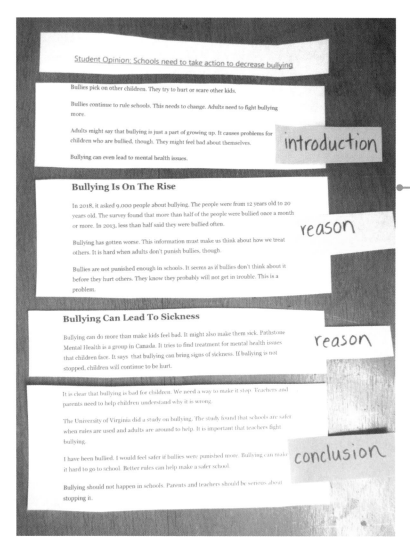

Materials used at a Writing station where students assemble an opinion piece, component by component, and use sticky notes to label each part.

4. Reflect With Students

After your students have worked with this timeless standard at the Writing station, reflect on what they've done here. Be sure to include a five- to ten-minute Reflection Time after stations where children can share what they learned as they worked together expressing opinions. You might also use the templates in Section 4 and the online companion to jot down your ideas about the work you and your children did. (There are printables in the online companion that you can also place at this station for students to use while cleaning up.)

Here are some questions to use during Reflection Time regarding the Writing station.

1. Name an opinion you wrote about at the Writing station today. What was your topic? Why did you choose that?

2. What is one reason you gave for your opinion?

3. Read a part where you used a transition word in your opinion writing (for Grades 2–4).

Timeless Writing Standard 5

Students will peer edit for punctuation, capitalization, spelling, and language conventions.

Let's take a look at this timeless standard before we begin teaching it in whole group and eventually moving it into a Writing station for practice. In this section, we will focus on helping kids learn and focus on *language conventions* by peer editing. Be sure to teach students how to revise or change their words to improve their writing, too, as part of this process. (See Timeless Writing Standard 2 for ideas on revision.)

Peer editing is sometimes also referred to as *peer conferencing* or *peer review*, but there are nuances. Revision and editing are two different parts of the writing process. Peer review and conferencing can help during both revision and editing, but peer editing often occurs during the final phase of writing when students are cleaning up language and conventions for clarity. Here we'll focus on peer editing, but many of these concepts can transfer to peer conferencing and peer review. Look closely at your own state standards for grade-level expectations and academic vocabulary to include as you teach.

What It Is

- In peer editing two students work together to read and improve their writing.

- A peer editor *helps* another writer make their writing clearer and helps them fix their mistakes in spelling, punctuation, capitalization, and usage.

- Peer editing involves complimenting, commenting, and correcting.

- Revision is about changing the content of writing—adding or deleting words, reorganizing ideas, or responding to a reader's questions. Editing focuses on conventions, such as punctuation, spelling, capitalization, and grammar. Writers revise *and* edit, and peers can be helpful in both.

Why It's Important

- Peer editing helps students learn to work together and to give and receive constructive feedback about their writing.

- Working with a partner to improve writing and fix errors provides a scaffold and a safety net. It's easier to do this with a classmate than alone. It's hard to see your own errors.

- Teaching someone else helps us learn. As we look at someone else's writing, it may help us think more carefully about our own work.

- Peer editing helps kids become independent of the teacher or another adult. Students learn to help each other rather than relying on the teacher for assistance.

- Reading and talking about their writing improves children's communication skills.

TIME-SAVING TIP: Teaching kids to peer edit can save teacher time in the long run. Students learn to fix their writing instead of asking you for help. This can improve writing and save you time while reading children's work.

Myths and Confusions

- Children sometimes confuse editing and revising. Help them understand what it means to edit and what it means to revise. Focus on revision first. Then move into editing using conventions. Be sure to spend more time on helping kids communicate their message with words than having them work on conventions.

- Instead of having kids try to fix everything at once, have them look for one convention at a time. For instance, I like to start with capitalization. We capitalize the first word in a sentence, young children's favorite word (*I*), as well as their names.

- Help students understand that writing conventions are for the *reader*, not the writer. Correctly spelled words, capital letters, punctuation, and grammar help readers understand what we've written. Conventions aren't just a bunch of rules to memorize. Writers use conventions to communicate messages clearly.

- At school, students often write just because the teacher said to. This makes writing (and editing) an assignment. Expanding audiences (beyond the teacher) to include other kids, family members, school personnel, authors of favorite books, and others in the community or world makes writing more personal and helps children to feel more ownership and excitement.

- Filling in blanks on worksheets doesn't teach kids to edit. It might be tested that way, but it often doesn't transfer. Teach conventions in context instead! Help students notice punctuation or capital letters in the books they read and the writing they do.

Real-World Connections

- Learning to work with others is a real-world skill. Being part of a team, cooperating, and giving or accepting feedback are important in the workplace.

- Writing emails or other correspondence is necessary in most adults' daily lives. Unedited or poorly edited writing can give the recipient an impression that the person who composed it is uneducated or not serious about their work.

- Editors work in many fields, including publishing, grant writing, and civic, scientific, or technical organizations. Editors are curious, creative, detail-oriented, and work well with others.

- As an author, I work with multiple editors—an editor who helps me formulate and revise ideas, a copy editor who reads for content and conventions, an editorial assistant who fact checks, and a production editor who manages all the processes of putting a book together.

How Practice at the Writing Station Helps Students

- Peer editing at the Writing station improves children's writing. The child who is the *writer* reads his writing to the other child acting as *editor*. This gives the writer a reason to read and hear his work, thus exposing things like missing words and punctuation.

- Choosing a specific convention to focus on with a partner helps both students become more aware of how periods, capital letters, or spelling helps their writing be better understood.

- It's more fun to look at your writing with a classmate than to have to figure out by yourself if your writing is your best.

- Using fun tools like stickers or colored pencils is motivating when working with a friend to help each other edit your writing at the Writing station.

It's important to teach concepts well in whole group before moving this work into the Writing station. This will help students to eventually know how to practice the same activities with a partner independently of you.

Work with conventions using model text and model sentences; then move into helping children look at their own writing during Writing Workshop. Let young writers work with the same picture books you've modeled with to practice talking about what they notice about how the authors used capital letters or nouns and verbs. Then have them do the same with their writing.

Remember there are a lot of moving parts to focus on related to writing conventions at each grade level. Examine your state standards and "stay in your lane!" Help kids get proficient with the pieces specified for your students' age and stage. I've included a sample Age- and Stage-Appropriate Conventions Chart for reference in the online companion.

Consider the following steps for student success with this standard.

1. Plan

Select Picture Books for Kids to Notice Writers' Conventions in Model Sentences

Because you'll be modeling the writing and editing work kids will do in the station, think about this standard and the kind of text that will help children understand the specific conventions you want them to learn. I recommend using model sentences within model texts to teach conventions.

Choose books that have examples of the conventions you're focusing on. For example, if you're working on end punctuation, choose a book that has periods, question marks, or exclamation points. If you are focusing on a spelling pattern like adding -s or -es, find books with examples of those kinds of words. Use these books at the Writing station for kids to use as references, too. You'll find model sentences in the lessons that follow on pages 145–152.

TIME-SAVING TIP: Work as a team to find mentor sentences that match what you'll be teaching. Save these examples in a file and return to them year after year to save time.

Because there are so many writing conventions to consider, I recommend taking it slow. Focus on one at a time. You might introduce the concept of why a convention, such as punctuation, is important by reading aloud a book written specifically to explain it. I've included in Section 4 lists of picture books to use to introduce concepts related to capitalization, punctuation, spelling, and grammar. A printable is available on the online companion, too, for you to give your librarian if you want help finding these titles.

Choose Which Writing Convention to Focus On

Be mindful as you approach writing conventions. Don't try to teach them all at once. Use your Writing station display area to post conventions your class is focusing on that you expect students to use. See the photo that follows for an example.

With young children, start with capitalization (focus especially on the pronoun, *I*, and the first letter of their names). Expect and remind kids to *speak* in sentences before expecting them to write sentences. Then move into end punctuation—periods, question marks, and exclamation points.

Older students can explore parts of speech and more complex sentence construction along with expanded use of punctuation (e.g., quotation marks and apostrophes) and capitalization (proper nouns, titles, historical periods and

EL TIP: Be sensitive to multilingual learners' understanding of and confusions with grammar and spelling. They are navigating between more than one language with different conventions. It may be helpful to show them a sentence constructed in their primary language with the same sentence in their new language. Ask them to notice what's the same and different.

events). I recommend Jeff Anderson and Whitney LaRocca's *Patterns of Power* (2017) for specifics in teaching language conventions using mentor sentences (with tons of mentor sentence examples). I've adapted some of their ideas in the lessons that follow.

Spelling can be a sticking point for some kids. They won't even try to write a word if they can't spell it correctly. Help students understand that spelling helps readers better understand their writing. It's a courtesy for the reader. Encourage young writers to write the sounds they hear in words. Start with expecting young kids to spell high-frequency words that you've taught using your word wall, as well as their names and those of their classmates. From there, help them try to use the first and last sounds of words. When children are reading at about a Fountas and Pinnell reading level C, expect them to spell CVC (consonant-vowel-consonant) words correctly (e.g., *hop, pig, bat*).

By the end of first grade and into second grade, help kids pay attention to the way words *look* as well as sound. And into third grade and up, work on word morphology—roots and origins of longer words. Connect your spelling instruction to kids' phonics learning. Understanding syllable types can be extremely helpful. (See *Simply Stations: Word Study* for more in-depth ideas on spelling instruction and related stations practice.)

Writing convention, capitalization, for kids to practice highlighted at the Writing station.

2. Teach

Teach Conventions Within the Context of Reading, Writing, and Speaking

Children will learn and remember more when they learn writing (and language) conventions in the context of reading, writing, and speaking. Instead of having kids cut and paste nouns and verbs on worksheets, have them speak and write in sentences. The purpose of learning the terms *noun* and *verb* is to give students language to use to talk about their writing. For example, *"A stronger verb will help the reader picture what you did."* Or, *"A proper noun will help the reader know exactly which park you went to on your picnic."* The lessons that follow give suggestions for teaching writing conventions in context rather than in isolation.

Model and Set Clear Expectations for Peer Editing

It's important to let kids know exactly what you expect them to do while peer editing. To clarify roles, students might wear nametags that say "Editor" and "Author." Printables can be found on the online companion, **resources.corwin .com/simplystations-writing**. Have two students show the class how to peer edit with a piece of their writing. Place the writing on a document camera while one student (the author) stands on the right and the editor stands on the left. Give the author a colored pencil. (The editor has no pencil.) Direct both students to look at the text while the author reads it to the editor. Then have *only the author* make changes, while the editor asks questions and makes suggestions. Remind the editor to ask the author why she used the convention you're working on (e.g., capital letters or noun-verb agreement) using the conversation cards.

Apply this procedure in the lessons that follow on pages 145–152. You might also make an anchor chart similar to the ones below to remind children how to peer edit. Post this at the Writing station after you've taught this procedure well.

How to Peer Edit anchor charts for younger students (left) and older kids (right).

Set Goals for Writing Conventions

Tell students what you want them to focus on as they edit their writing. Say, *As you read your writing today, look for end punctuation. Did you stop? There should be a period. Or did you pause? That's a comma.*

Use a conversation card such as *I put a period here because* _____ or *I put a question mark here because* _____.

Co-Create Anchor Charts to Help Students Remember

Work with students to make anchor charts that help them remember when to use capital letters or end punctuation. Ditto for spelling and language usage. As you make each chart include the following:

- A title telling which convention you're focusing on

- A sentence you've taught with showing where the convention fits

- A bright color highlighting the convention

Here are some sample charts for inspiration:

Anchor charts for conventions.

On the following pages are two sample lessons for modeling you can use when teaching children about peer editing using conventions. One lesson is for primary grades and focuses on capital letters; the other is for Grades 2–4 and examines noun-verb agreement. Use these as examples to get you started with strong whole group lessons that will be transferred to partner practice at the Writing station over time.

The goal is for students eventually to work with a partner to read and edit their writing, applying appropriate conventions to improve communication. I included sample texts, but feel free to use your own.

SAMPLE WRITING LESSON WITH A MODEL TEXT in PRIMARY GRADES

MODEL TEXT: *My Name Is Elizabeth* by Annika Dunklee (a story young children can connect to that includes names and has simple text)

TIMELESS STANDARD: Students will peer edit for capitalization. (Adjust this, as needed, to match your state and grade-level standards.)

TEACHER TALK:

- Writers use capital letters to show importance.

- Capital letters get our attention. Authors use them to start sentences, and to start names of special people, places, and things.

- Sometimes writers use all capital letters in a word. Say that word loudly with feeling!

- Editors help writers fix their writing.

STUDENT TALK: Use the conversation card to demonstrate. (An example of the printable is on page 169, and you can download it from the online companion to use with your students.) Kids will use these in whole group and over time at the Writing station, too.

- I see a **capital letter**. Why did you put it here?

LESSON STEPS:

You might break this lesson into two or three days when first introducing these ideas.

1. Read aloud the model text during reading time. Revisit it on another day during Writing Workshop.

2. Tell students that authors think about using capital letters when they write. They use capital letters to show importance.

3. Look through the book together, paying attention to where the author used capital letters. Invite children to tell you what they notice using the conversation card and answering the question. (e.g., *I see a capital letter, M. Why did you put it here? It's the first word in the sentence.* Or, *I see a capital letter, E. Why did you put it here? It's the first letter in Elizabeth's name.*)

4. Make an anchor chart about using capital letters, as shown in the photo on the facing page.

5. Have two children model peer editing using their writing and a document camera, as described on page 143. Have them look for capital letters together and talk about where these are used and why. Give the author a green pencil to mark capital letters. If a capital letter is needed, have the author underline the letter with a green line. Some students may enjoy playing editor by using editing marks that adults use. (See the example anchor chart on page 147.)

6. After the modeling, review why writers use capital letters. Then pair all students and have them work together to peer edit for capitals in a similar way. Give each author a green pencil. Circulate among them as they work, paying attention to their understanding and confusions.

7. End with a brief sharing time where several pairs share their writing and what they noticed about capital letters.

QUICK ASSESS:

What did children notice about the use of capital letters? Were they able to tell why the author used these (beginning of a sentence, first letter in a person's name, the word *I*, for emphasis)? Did students use capital letters? Could they tell why they used a capital letter in their writing? Did they work together to help each other talk about capital letters?

AUTHOR'S CRAFT CONNECTION:

On another day, use author's craft cards to think about words in which the author used *all* capital letters. (A matching printable can be found on the companion website.) The goal is for students to understand this well enough that they can eventually do this without teacher assistance at the Writing station.

● Find a place where the author used all capital letters in a word. Why do you think she did this?

● Find a place in your writing where you might use all capital letters in a word. Why would you do this here?

READING CONNECTION:

Ask students to pay attention to capital letters as they read independently. Have them share examples of how authors used capital letters in the word *I* or at the beginning of a sentence or to show a special name. They might add sticky notes with examples from their reading to your anchor chart on capitalization.

MOVING THIS LESSON TO PARTNER PRACTICE AT A STATION:

Place the Author and Editor tags and one green colored pencil at the Writing station for students to use as they peer edit for capital letters. Post and review your expectations for peer editing. Remind kids that they can work together on a piece they wrote on a different day. Or they can write for a while and then peer edit. They might also want to look at the model texts or books from independent reading for examples of places where authors used capital letters.

Grades K–1 anchor chart about capitalization.

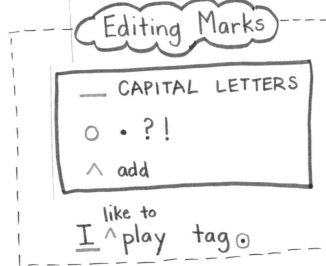

Grades K–1 anchor chart of simple editing marks.

SAMPLE WRITING LESSON WITH A MODEL TEXT in INTERMEDIATE GRADES

MODEL TEXT: *The Branch* by Mireille Messier (a picture book with a few two-word sentences in it for Grades 2–4)

TIMELESS STANDARD: Students will peer edit for noun-verb agreement. (Adjust this, as needed, to match your state and grade-level standards.)

TEACHER TALK:

- Editors work with authors to make their writing the best it can be.

- Nouns and verbs must agree. This helps the reader understand the writer's message.

- How do you know the nouns and verbs get along?

- Be sure your nouns and verbs sound right.

- Is the noun singular or plural (shows more than one person, place, or thing)? How do you know? What does the verb do to agree with the noun?

STUDENT TALK:

Use the conversation cards to demonstrate. (Printables are found in the online companion.) Kids will use these in whole group and over time at the Writing station, too.

- I'm the **author**. I read my writing aloud and look and listen. I make changes as needed.

- I'm the **editor**. I look at and listen to the writing. I make suggestions of things to fix.

- I look and listen for the **nouns** and **verbs** in a **sentence**. Do they **agree**? Do they **sound** right? Do they **look** right?

- The **noun** (or **pronoun**) is _____. It **agrees** with the **verb**, _____.

- _____ is a _____ **noun** (or **pronoun**). (**singular/plural**)

    It **agrees** with the **verb**, _____.

LESSON STEPS:

1. Read aloud the model text before using it in this lesson, so students are familiar with this book when you return to it during writing time.

2. Tell the class that today they will learn to be editors. Editors work with authors to make their writing better. Explain that authors and editors use special vocabulary, like *nouns* and *verbs*, to talk about writing.

3. Ask kids what they know about nouns and verbs and chart a few of their ideas for reference. (See photo on the following page.) If they don't mention nouns and verbs matching or agreeing, add this to the chart. Explain that the nouns and verbs in a sentence need to look right *and* sound right. You might also include *pronouns* because many sentences, such as the two-word examples that follow, include them.

4. Show the model text and find a page that has several two-word sentences on it. (Start with two-word sentences to simplify noun-verb agreement.) Write those sentences on the board for kids to examine. Ask what they noticed using the conversation cards, such as *"The noun (or pronoun) is 'I.' It agrees with the verb, concentrate."*

   I concentrate. I squint. And then, I have an idea!

5. Tell students you'd like them to work in pairs to look for noun-verb agreement in their writing; one will be the author and the other the editor. Have two kids model how to peer edit using the procedure on page 143. You might have them find the verb first and underline it lightly in blue. Then have them find and underline the noun before it in green and check that these words agree when reading just those two aloud. For example, in the sentence, *Darla walked to the store,* children would underline *walked* and *Darla.* Then they'd say, "Darla walked" to check for noun-verb agreement.

6. Have children work together as author and editor pairs around the room, looking and listening to each other's writing. Move around the classroom, supporting students as needed. End with a brief sharing time where several pairs share examples of noun-verb agreement they found or fixed in each other's writing.

7. The next day, repeat this process. This time, share a longer sentence from the book to talk about as editors. For example, *Mom stands next to me at the window.* Again have students use the conversation cards to talk about noun-verb agreement: *"The first noun is 'Mom.' It agrees with the verb, 'stands.'" It sounds right—'Mom stands.'"* Ask kids to work in author-editor pairs to continue to help each other with noun-verb agreement in their writing.

8. Once students understand how to look and listen for noun-verb agreement, add the terms *singular* and *plural nouns* to their talk about writing. Use the matching conversation cards and examples from the model text. Help kids notice that plural nouns usually end in *-s, -es,* or *-ies,* but the matching verbs don't! Have them continue to peer edit together and use this new academic vocabulary as they talk about their sentences.

What third graders knew about nouns and verbs.

Anchor chart on noun-verb agreement.

QUICK ASSESS:

Could students find nouns and verbs in model text sentences? Did they understand what noun-verb agreement means? Were they able to follow peer editing expectations and work together to help each other fix up their writing? Did they use academic vocabulary, including *noun*, *verb*, *noun-verb agreement*, *singular noun*, *plural noun*?

AUTHOR'S CRAFT CONNECTION:

On another day use author's craft cards to help students think about how writers vary sentence length but still include nouns and verbs in agreement. (A matching printable can be found in the online companion.) The goal is for students to understand this well enough that they can eventually do this without teacher assistance at the Writing station.

- Pick a page and read it, paying attention to the sentences. Are all the sentences long? Are they all short? Or are there some of both?

- Choose a short sentence. Does it have a noun and verb and how do they agree?

- Choose a long sentence. Does it have nouns and verbs and how do they agree?

READING CONNECTION:

Don't ask students to find nouns and verbs while reading independently or in small group. This will get in the way of their comprehension. As children read and talk about text they're reading, remind them to *speak in sentences* about what they read. This will help them *use* nouns and verbs in agreement.

After kids have read a book, they might look for nouns and verbs to study author's craft which will help them as writers. Have them use the conversation cards or the author's craft cards used in the above lesson.

MOVING THIS LESSON TO PARTNER PRACTICE AT A STATION:

At the Writing station, have kids work with a classmate using the same tools you used in whole group. Have partners work together as Editor and Author to read and edit for noun-verb agreement. They might like to wear the printable nametags found in the online companion to define their roles. Display anchor charts on noun-verb agreement and peer editing for students to use as resources while working at the Writing station. They can use the author's craft card to discuss model texts and review what they've learned about noun-verb agreement.

3. Partner Practice

Once you see that students are able to peer edit for noun-verb agreement in whole group, you're ready to move that same work into partner practice at the Writing station.

Remember to provide all the tools you used to teach this concept in whole group. These will remind children of the important thinking and discussion you expect them to have at this station. I've included additional grade-specific suggestions to help you think about the best things for your children to practice.

Kindergarten

- It's not important for kindergartners to find nouns and verbs in text. These grammatical terms are very abstract for young children. However, it is important for young children to *speak* in sentences, *using* nouns and verbs as they talk about what they're writing (and reading).

- Kindergartners can peer edit for capital letters. They can also edit for end punctuation. At first, have them check for a period at the end of their writing. They will often place periods at the end of each line. (Eventually they will learn to have a punctuation mark at the end of each sentence.) Over time, they can also edit for spaces between words. This happens more easily when they have one-to-one matching and understand what a word is. By the end of the year, they can edit for spelling high-frequency words (e.g., *I, my, like, can, go*) by using a word wall.

- Little kids will enjoy making short sentences by putting words together on a pocket chart. You might label one side "who" (*naming words*) and the other side "what they do" (*action words*) as done below. Then have kids make up two-word sentences with these words. Provide words they can read. Add picture support to cards to help children just learning to read. Here's a list of suggested words:

WHO (NAMING WORDS)	WHAT THEY DO (ACTION WORDS)
names of students	hop
I	run
you	go
we	swim
dogs	sit
cats	play
frogs	nap

After kids make sentences by putting two words together that sound right, have them copy their sentence and add an illustration. Then ask them to be editors and add more details to their sentence. Also have them use conversation cards from the primary lesson on page 145. Did they use a capital letter at the beginning? Did they use a period at the end? When they can do this in whole group, move this as an option to the kindergarten Writing station.

Grades 1–2

- First and second graders should be expected to speak in sentences. This will get them in the habit of *using* nouns and verbs rather than just identifying these parts of speech.

- In first grade, you might talk with kids about "words that name" before introducing the abstract term, *noun*. Ditto with "words that show action" before calling them *verbs*. The emphasis should be on helping kids use these terms to *talk* about their writing at the sentence level. Here are a few examples of what you might say to model this:

  ○ "Ezra Jack Keats used the verb *stretched* to help us picture Peter reaching really high as he built with blocks in *Peter's Chair*."

  ○ "This author used *proper nouns* to name the characters Peter and Susie. That helps us get to know them better than if he called them *the little boy* and *the little girl*."

○ "As you edit, think about the nouns you used. Do they name people, places, and things in a way that helps your reader picture them? Do your verbs show strong actions?"

● Have first and second graders work together to peer edit for noun-verb agreement without using this term. Use these words instead: *Read a sentence. Listen. Do the words sound right? Look. Did you put the endings on all the words? Check for -s at the end.*

Grades 3–4

● Students in upper grades are ready for more advanced grammatical terms and concepts, such as *compound sentences* and *prepositional phrases* because they can think more abstractly. Use academic vocabulary and expect kids to do the same as they talk about their writing with each other as editors. Check your grade-level standards for exact terms.

● Expand children's work with noun-verb agreement to *compound sentences* over time. In whole group, use model sentences (from model text) to examine how authors combine two sentences with the words *for, and not, but, or, yet, so* (often remembered by the acronym, FANBOYS), and use a comma. Ask students to identify each sentence and check each side of the comma for noun-verb agreement. You might rewrite the model sentence with other verbs and have kids compare versions to see which is correct and tell why.

> *I try to pick up my branch, but it is too heavy.* (from the model text)
>
> *I tried to pick up my branch, but it is too heavy.*
>
> *I tries to pick my branch, but it was too heavy.*

Then have partners look in their own writing for examples of compound sentences and noun-verb agreement, working together as author and editor. When they know how to do this, add this task to the We Can list at the Writing station.

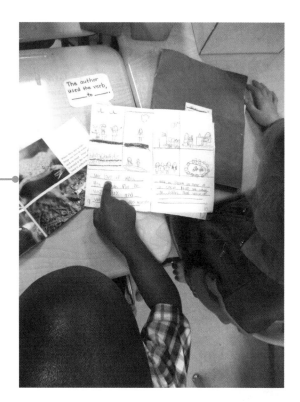

Partners use a conversation card to talk about verbs in their writing and in a book.

4. Reflect With Students

After your students have worked with this timeless standard at the Writing station, reflect on what they've done here. Be sure to include a five- to ten-minute Reflection Time after stations where children can share what they learned as they edited with a peer for conventions. You might also refer to the templates in Section 4 and printables in the online companion (**resources.corwin.com/simplystations-writing**) to record your ideas about the work you and your children did.

Children may use the questions below to talk about the peer editing work they did at the Writing station. Older students might use the printable reflection questions found in the online companion to discuss what they learned as they clean up. Use these questions with the class during Reflection Time, too.

1. What did you and your partner look for while peer editing?

2. Tell something you fixed up while peer editing your writing today.

3. What did you learn when peer editing that you'll try to remember to do every time you write?

4

Reflection, Printables, and Resources

This section is designed to provide a visual index of everything you need to keep the Writing station working well as your students grow more independent throughout the school year. All of the printable materials are in English and Spanish and can be downloaded from the online companion, located at **resources .corwin.com/simplystations-writing**.

We start with questions to use for personal **reflection**, things to discuss in Professional Learning Community (PLC) or data team meetings with your grade level, and questions for students to use when thinking about their work at this station.

resources.corwin.com/
simplystations-writing

Next you'll find **printable** tools to help you get started with stations: icons for the management board and matching signs, planning calendars to use when introducing and rolling out stations, and a checklist of routines to model for the Writing station. I've designed several choices of paper, based on ages and stages of writing development, as well as an Early Developmental Writing Stages chart you can share with parents. Also included are thumbnails of printable pages that match the sample lessons for modeling and suggestions from Section 3 of this book. Online you will find several blank forms for conversation cards to personalize and make your own, based on your state standards and academic vocabulary.

Finally, in this section I've provided **resources** for materials you might use at the Writing station, including ideas for word banks and seasonal writing. You'll find digital options for planning and storing student writing, and suggested titles for model texts to use as you teach kids to write stories, informational text, and opinion pieces. There are also lists of picture books you might use to introduce punctuation, capitalization, and language conventions across the grades. The final chart includes a bibliography of all the books used in the lessons in Section 3.

I'd love to hear from you about resources you use for this station, too. Please use the hashtag #simplystations on social media. You can find me online at the following:

@debbiediller (Twitter)

debbie.diller (Instagram)

dillerdebbie (Facebook)

www.debbiediller.com (website)

Reflection Tools

Here are some questions to reflect on across the school year, after your students have been working at the Writing station for a while. The companion website, **resources.corwin.com/simplystations-writing**, contains printables of reflection tools for teacher use, PLC use, and student use at stations and in wrap-up time. Use these pages to record what you've tried, what's worked, and what you might change in the future. I recommend making three copies of this reflection sheet and filling it in at the beginning, middle, and end of the school year, or at the end of each term.

[Teacher Reflection]

After your students have been working at the Writing station for a while, here are some questions to reflect on across the school year. Use this page to record what you've tried, what's worked, and what you might change in the future. I recommend making three copies of this reflection sheet, and fillin[...] and end of the school year, or at the end of each term.

1. Use this rubric to evaluate how this station is working after you introduce [...] your Writing station work?

Students write or talk about their writing the whole time		
Kids use writing resources (samples, charts, word banks)		
Writing improves over time		
Children apply craft and conventions being studied		
Students are eager to use the Writing station		
	1	**2**
	Not Well	

2. Based on your ratings above, which area do you want to focus on to improv[...]

3. What will you add or change to help students better utilize the Writing sta[...]

4. Observe students in this station. What do they spend most of their time d[...] most engaged? Least? What could you add to get or keep them writing?

[PLC Reflection]

1. Do you have a Writing station? Why or why not? Is it stationary or portable? Why?

2. What are your students currently practicing at the Writing station? How is it related to what you've taught in whole group writing? What standard does it connect to?

3. Answer these questions and share with your team. Is there consistency across your grade level?

Do students regularly write with purpose and voice at a Writing station?	YES	NO
Do you have options for them to choose what to write about at this station?	YES	NO
Are you planning writing instruction as a team and seeing students apply what you've been teaching them to do as writers at this station?	YES	NO

4. Bring samples of writing your students have produced at the Writing station to a data meeting. Include writing from different developmental levels represented in your class. As a team, sort the samples into writing levels. Use the Early Developmental Writing Stages chart as a reference for students writing at emergent stages. Then make a list of what students have done well at each level. Brainstorm what is the next step to help kids improve as writers at each level.

(Continued)

Student Reflection Cards

I recommend that you save about five to ten minutes each day for Reflection Time after stations and small group time. Have your students meet in the whole group meeting area and talk with them about a few stations they worked at that day. This will provide "paperless accountability" and lets children know you care about what they practiced and learned today. It also will help you troubleshoot and provide ongoing positive reminders about what to do at stations. You won't have time to ask kids about every station every day. So choose just one or two stations to reflect on each day. I recommend starting with the Writing station, especially if you find that students aren't producing high-quality work here. Having an audience for their writing usually brings about improvement quickly!

TIME-SAVING TIP: Print all the reflection cards for the Writing station onto cardstock. Hole-punch them in the upper left-hand corner and place them on a 1" book ring for ease of use. Keep them in your whole group teaching area for quick reference.

On the companion website, you'll find a set of printable reflection cards to use *following* stations and small group to discuss the Writing station. Each matches a timeless standard for partner reading from Section 3. I've labeled them for ease of use. Timeless Standard 1 is TS1, and so on.

You might also place a copy of a reflection card matching the standard kids are practicing at the Writing station for writers to use as they are cleaning up. (I wouldn't place these at the station in Grades K–1, because most students won't be able to read them.)

HOW to USE REFLECTION CARDS

1. Gather your class to the carpet following stations and small group time for Reflection Time.

2. Choose a few stations to discuss. Start with the Writing station if you'd like kids to improve here.

3. Use a reflection card to match what kids have been practicing at that station.

4. Ask one or two questions from the card.

5. Repeat with a reflection card to match practice at another station.

1. What did you write about at the Writing station today? How did you come up with your idea?

2. How did you plan your writing at the Writing station today? What did you use to get started?

3. Who was your audience for what you wrote today? Why did you write this piece?

TS1

Planning Tools

TIME-SAVING TIP:
A master calendar will help you plan when to introduce and refresh each station. If you have others on your grade level, plan and work together to simplify the rollout of each station.

As noted in Section 2, plotting out when you'll introduce each station throughout the first few weeks of school helps smooth implementation. Also plan for a "reboot" periodically where you'll commit to looking closer at what students are doing at that station. Be ready to add, change, or replace things at that time.

The **Roll-Out Calendar for Introducing and Refreshing Stations** can be invaluable for planning. See pages 16–17 for a sample filled-in calendar. Remember to recycle things from whole group into stations, so you can work smarter, not harder. You can find a printable, blank calendar on the companion website, **resources.corwin.com/simplystations-writing**.

Roll-Out Calendar
for Introducing and Refreshing Stations

AUGUST
- Week 1
- Week 2
- Week 3
- Week 4

SEPTEMBER
- Week 1
- Week 2
- Week 3
- Week 4

OCTOBER
- Week 1
- Week 2
- Week 3
- Week 4

NOVEMBER
- Week 1
- Week 2
- Week 3
- Week 4

DECEMBER

JANUARY
- Week 1
- Week 2
- Week 3
- Week 4

FEBRUARY

NOTES

Use the **Checklist of Routines** to help you remember to model everything needed for children to be successful at the Writing station. There's a space to jot notes and reflect on how your Launch Lessons went for future reference.

Use the **Simply Stations Planning Tool** when planning instruction from standards to stations. I recommend working with a team to do this. Also see Section 3, pages 50–51, for suggestions for using this tool individually or with your team.

Checklist *of* Routines

to Model and Expect at the Writing Station

Use this checklist to help you remember to model everything needed for children to be successful with independent writing time and at the Writing station. There's a space to jot notes and reflect on how your launch lessons went for future reference.

Writing Routines: MODEL HOW TO . . .

ROUTINE MODELED	DATE INTRODUCED	MY NOTES
Choose a writing idea you know and care about		
Choose paper and writing materials		
Think about audience		
Think about purpose for writing this piece		
Use resources (e.g., writing samples, charts, dictionaries, model texts)		
Work in a designated spot		
Write something; make one of something (don't waste time or materials)		
Write alone or with a partner		
Talk about your writing with a partner (e.g., planning, responding, editing)		
Peer edit using writing tools and charts		
Put writing and other materials away (clean up)		

Simply Stations Planning Tool

Standards to Stations

STANDARD WE'RE TEACHING	ACADEMIC VOCABULARY	WHOLE GROUP IDEAS	PARTNER PRACTICE AT LITERACY STATIONS
			_____ Station
			→

The **Early Developmental Writing Stages** chart can help you carefully consider the levels at which your students are writing so you can plan lessons and stations that meet them where they are and guide them to the next level. This chart can help you examine what kids *can* do as young writers. It's designed to show where they are on a writing continuum, much as you'd look at their reading levels. In a kindergarten or first-grade classroom you may have students still writing at very early stages, because they have not had opportunities to play with writing materials. Thus, I've included writing materials that best match their needs.

Use this chart to identify where kids are and think about next moves for them as writers. For example, a child at the mock letter stage should not be expected to write on lined paper and represent sounds with matching letters—even if that child can identify some letters and say their sounds. Writing requires fine motor control as well as hearing and representing sounds.

Share the Early Developmental Writing Stages chart with parents and caregivers as you confer with them. Look together at samples of their child's writing and help them identify the stage the child is in. Help adults understand that children who are scribbling and drawing letter-like shapes are writing. Encourage them to provide opportunities for their young ones to "write" by making a grocery list or a card for someone they know.

Download blank, full-size, printable planning tools from the companion website, **resources.corwin.com/simplystations-writing**.

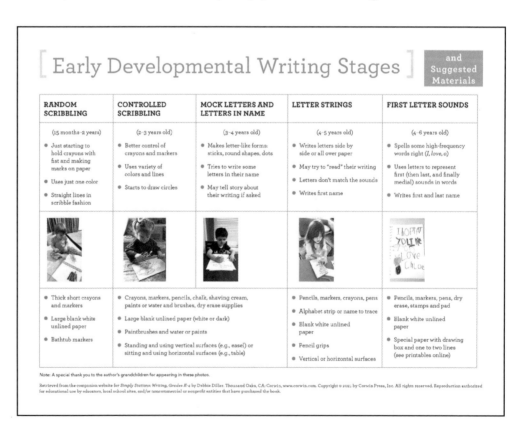

[Early Developmental Writing Stages] and Suggested Materials

RANDOM SCRIBBLING	CONTROLLED SCRIBBLING	MOCK LETTERS AND LETTERS IN NAME	LETTER STRINGS	FIRST LETTER SOUNDS
(15 months–2 years)	(2–3 years old)	(3–4 years old)	(4–5 years old)	(4–6 years old)
• Just starting to hold crayons with fist and making marks on paper • Uses just one color • Straight lines in scribble fashion	• Better control of crayons and markers • Uses variety of colors and lines • Starts to draw circles	• Makes letter-like forms: sticks, round shapes, dots • Tries to write some letters in their name • May tell story about their writing if asked	• Writes letters side by side or all over paper • May try to "read" their writing • Letters don't match the sounds • Writes first name	• Spells some high-frequency words right (I, love, a) • Uses letters to represent first (then last, and finally medial) sounds in words • Writes first and last name
• Thick short crayons and markers • Large blank white unlined paper • Bathtub markers	• Crayons, markers, pencils, chalk, shaving cream, paints or water and brushes, dry erase supplies • Large blank unlined paper (white or dark) • Paintbrushes and water or paints • Standing and using vertical surfaces (e.g., easel) or sitting and using horizontal surfaces (e.g., table)		• Pencils, markers, crayons, pens • Alphabet strip or name to trace • Blank white unlined paper • Pencil grips • Vertical or horizontal surfaces	• Pencils, markers, pens, dry erase, stamps and pad • Blank white unlined paper • Special paper with drawing box and one to two lines (see printables online)

Note: A special thank you to the author's grandchildren for appearing in these photos.

Printable Tools for Teaching and Transfer

The companion website, **resources.corwin.com/simplystations-writing**, contains full-page printables in English and Spanish that match the items needed for the lessons found in Section 3 of this book. Use them when teaching in whole and small group, where appropriate. Then transfer them to the Writing station. The online printables are organized by timeless standard to make them easy to find. You'll find all of these items in full-page printable format on the companion website, but here I'll just show thumbnails of the items by type, to give you a visual guide of what you'll find online.

Timeless Writing Standard 1
Conversation Cards for Generating Ideas and Making a Plan: Grades K–1, Grades 2–4
Author's Craft Cards for Generating Ideas and Making a Plan: Grades K–1, Grades 2–4
Planning Maps: Heart Map, Bone Map, Brain Map
Story Writing Plan for Primary Grades
Grades K–1 Word Banks: Family Words, Place We Go

Timeless Writing Standard 2
Conversation Cards for Writing and Revising Stories: Grades K–1, Grades 2–4
Author's Craft Cards for Writing and Revising Stories: Grades K–1, Grades 2–4
Comic Writing Template
Storyboard for Intermediate Grades

Timeless Writing Standard 3
Conversation Cards for Writing and Organizing Informational Texts: Grades K–1, Grades 2–4
Author's Craft Cards for Writing and Organizing Informational Texts: Grades K–1, Grades 2–4
Graphic Organizers: Circle Map, Tree Map
Letter-Writing Station: I Can List

Timeless Writing Standard 4
Conversation Cards for Writing to Express Opinions: Grades K–1, Grades 2–4
Author's Craft Cards for Writing to Express Opinions: Grades K–1, Grades 2–4
Planning for Opinion Writing
Words to Use When Expressing Opinions

Timeless Writing Standard 5
Conversation Cards for Peer Editing for Conventions: Grades K–1, Grades 2–4
Author's Craft Cards for Peer Editing for Conventions: Grades K–1, Grades 2–4
Age- and Stage-Appropriate Conventions Chart
Editor and Author Nametags
Paper Choices: Grades K–1 Picture Writing Paper, Grade 1 Picture Writing Paper, Grade 1 Picture Drawing Paper With Handwriting Lines
My Writing Goals: Narrative, Informational Text, Opinion
Think-Write-Read Graphic

Icons and Signs

The companion website, **resources.corwin.com/simplystations-writing**, includes printable icon cards for your management board and full-page foldable signs for each station.

You can use these icons and matching signs to label spaces around the room where students will work at literacy stations. This will help learners know where to go quickly and easily.

Listening and Speaking Station

Independent Reading Station

Partner Reading Station

Writing Station

Poetry Station

Drama Station

Word Study Station

Inquiry and Research Station

Let's Talk Station

Letter Writing Station

Meet With Teacher

Conversation Cards

for Generating Ideas and Making a Plan

The companion website, **resources.corwin.com/simplystations-writing**, contains larger printables of every conversation card to use in each of the timeless standards lessons and at stations when children practice the skills. Model how to use these cards in whole group before ever moving them into the Writing station. Remember, you can modify these cards according to your students' needs and your standards.

GRADES K–1 CONVERSATION CARD EXAMPLE

I will write about _____.

iStock.com/hayatikayhan

TS1

GRADES 2–4 CONVERSATION CARD EXAMPLES

I'm going to write about _____ because _____.

TS1

My **topic** is _____. I narrowed it down to focus on _____.

TS1

Conversation Cards

for Writing and Revising Stories

The companion website, **resources.corwin.com/simplystations-writing**, contains larger printables of every conversation card to use in each of the timeless standards lessons and at stations when children practice the skills. Model how to use these cards in whole group before ever moving them into the Writing station. Remember, you can modify these cards according to your students' needs and your standards.

GRADES K–1 CONVERSATION CARD EXAMPLE

My story is **in order. First . . . then . . . next . . . at the end . . . .**

First . . .	Then . . . Next . . .	At the end . . .

TS2

GRADES 2–4 CONVERSATION CARD EXAMPLES

I added the **detail** _____
to help my readers _____
_____ .

TS2

I **revised** my story to
make the part about
_____ clearer.

TS2

Conversation Cards

for Writing and Organizing Informational Texts

The companion website, **resources.corwin.com/simplystations-writing**, contains larger printables of every conversation card to use in each of the timeless standards lessons and at stations when children practice the skills. Model how to use these cards in whole group before ever moving them into the Writing station. Remember, you can modify these cards according to your students' needs and your standards.

GRADES K–1 CONVERSATION CARD EXAMPLE

My **topic** is _____.

iStock.com/iridi

TS3

GRADES 2–4 CONVERSATION CARD EXAMPLES

My **topic** is _____,
and all the information I've
included goes with it.

TS3

In this part I'm **describing**
_____.

TS3

Conversation Cards

The companion website, **resources.corwin.com/simplystations-writing**, contains larger printables of every conversation card to use in each of the timeless standards lessons and at stations when children practice the skills. Model how to use these cards in whole group before ever moving them into the Writing station. Remember, you can modify these cards according to your students' needs and your standards.

GRADES K–1 CONVERSATION CARD EXAMPLE

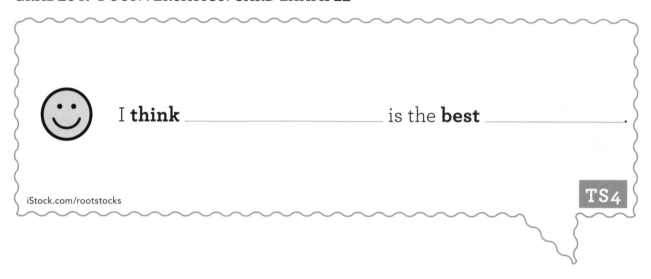

I **think** _____ is the **best** _____.

iStock.com/rootstocks

TS4

GRADES 2–4 CONVERSATION CARD EXAMPLES

In my **opinion**, I think that
_____.

One reason for this is
_____.

Another reason is
_____.

TS4

This is why I think that

_____.

TS4

Conversation Cards

for Peer Editing for Conventions

The companion website, **resources.corwin.com/simplystations-writing**, contains larger printables of every conversation card to use in each of the timeless standards lessons and at stations when children practice the skills. Model how to use these cards in whole group before ever moving them into the Writing station. Remember, you can modify these cards according to your students' needs and your standards.

GRADES K–1 CONVERSATION CARD EXAMPLE

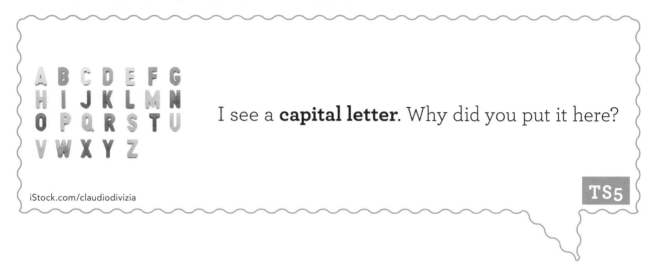

I see a **capital letter**. Why did you put it here?

iStock.com/claudiodivizia

TS5

GRADES 2–4 CONVERSATION CARD EXAMPLES

I'm the **author**. I read my writing aloud and look and listen. I make changes as needed.

TS5

I'm the **editor**. I look at and listen to the writing. I make suggestions of things to fix.

TS5

Author's Craft Cards

Author's craft cards can be used to help students examine text and use what they learned while writing. Model how to use these cards in whole group before moving them to the Writing station. Full-size printables of the author's craft cards for each timeless standard can be downloaded from the companion website, **resources .corwin.com/simplystations-writing**. You'll find them organized by timeless standard, then by grade band.

GRADES K–1 AUTHOR'S CRAFT CARD EXAMPLES

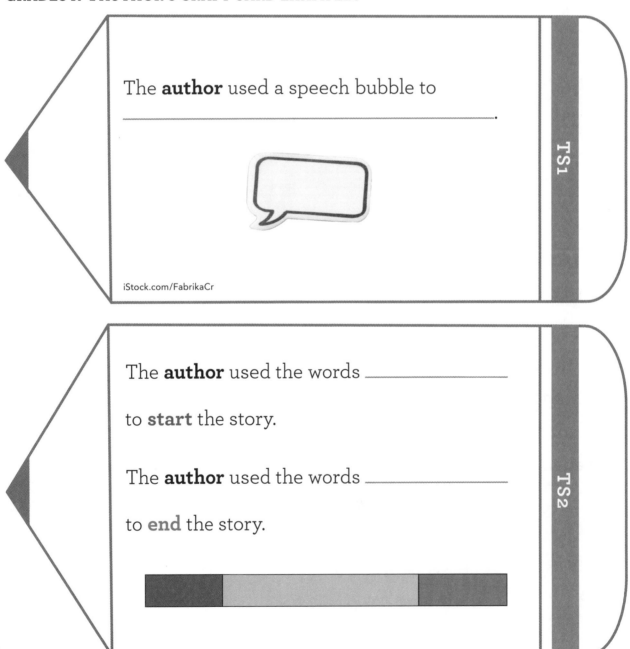

The **author** used a speech bubble to

_____ .

iStock.com/FabrikaCr

TS1

The **author** used the words _____

to **start** the story.

The **author** used the words _____

to **end** the story.

TS2

- What **form** did the author use to write? (e.g., poem with stanzas)

- Look at the **author's** use of **punctuation**, especially **questions**. How can questions help you as a writer?

- Examine the **illustrations**. What ideas do they give you as a writer?

TS1

- Choose a page. Find **descriptive details** the **author** used. Cover them with sticky notes. Read the story. How does it sound?

- Find **descriptive words** in the story that tell when something happened. What does this help you picture?

- Find **details** in the story that tell where something happened. What do you see in your mind?

- Look for **adjectives** on a page. What do they help you better picture? Does every sentence have them?

TS2

Paper Choices

What is the best paper for students to write on? Big paper, small paper, lined or unlined, fancy or plain? Over the years, I've learned that simple is best. Avoid lots of doodads and busy borders. Let kids add their own if they'd like! I've included samples of Grades K–1 writing paper in the online companion that you can print and use with your students, especially for those in kindergarten at early stages. See recommendations below for what kind of paper to use and why across the grade levels.

WRITING STAGE	WHAT KIND OF PAPER?	WHY?
Scribbling (random and controlled)	• Blank unlined 8½-x-11 or larger • White, manila, or light colors	• Lines get in the way and may confuse our youngest writers.
Mock Letters and Letter Strings	• Blank unlined 9-x-12 or smaller • White, manila, or light colors • Black or dark colors (for writing with chalk) • Folded paper for cards (fold 8½-x-11 paper in half) • Blank white unlined strips for lists (4¼-x-11)	• Large surfaces give them more room to explore. • Light-colored paper lets them see marks they made. • Dark-colored paper is a fun, new option with chalk as fine motor skills improve. • Making cards and lists gives a sense of purpose for early writers.
First Letter Sounds	 	• Paper with a box and a line or two helps children think about space on the page as they compose. • Too many lines confuse young writers. • Simple paper doesn't distract kids.

1st Graders (not at the above levels)		Children at this level know more about letters and their formation and can think about placing their letters on lines.
	iStock.com/Mai Vu	Landscape orientation encourages young writers to write more (as they fill lines going across).
		You may use paper like this with a drawing box at the top, too.
2nd Graders		Students are gaining fine motor control and can write on smaller spaces.
		Baselines and midlines still help them with correct letter placement on the page.
	iStock.com/Mai Vu	
3rd and 4th Graders		Students know more about letter formation and don't need baseline, midline, and top line guidance.
		You might have them write on every other line, so they have room for revising and editing.
	iStock.com/bombuscreative	

Letter Writing Station Ideas

Writing letters and making cards and notes give kids authentic purposes and audiences for writing. Who doesn't love to get mail? To increase writing motivation, you might periodically set up a specialized Writing station called the Letter Writing station. They can do everything from writing notes to each other (and you) to making birthday or get-well cards.

In Timeless Standard 4 we helped students write to express opinions, encouraging kids to be advocates. At a Letter Writing station, little ones can write postcards with just one to two lines and a drawing; older kids can write letters and/or emails and even compose tweets that the teacher can send from a class account about topics of concern to them.

Here are some ideas to get you started with a Letter Writing station, including what you'll need and what partners might do at this station. (You'll find a special icon for this station in the online companion, too.) Model well before releasing partners to work here independently of you. Also, find a way to mail (or email) students' letters and notes, so they will get responses.

Materials Needed for a Letter Writing Station

- Paper (letter writing printable on the online companion)

- Envelopes

- 4-x-6 index cards (for postcards)

- Samples of letters written by your class

- Real greeting cards (ask relatives for old or blank cards)

- Construction paper folded to make cards that fit your envelopes

- Samples of greeting card sentiments (to help with spelling; e.g., *happy birthday, congratulations, in sympathy*)

- Pencils and pens

- Markers for making cards

- Names and addresses of people to write to (make with your class, as needed)

I Can List for the Letter Writing Station

Post clear expectations for what students can do as they write alone or with a partner at the Letter Writing station. Add illustrations, as shown below, for Grades K–1 students.

I can:

- **Write a letter**
- **Write a postcard**
- **Make a card**

iStock.com/Fayethequeen; iStock.com/Plisman

For upper grades, include advocacy ideas on your I Can list. Here's a sample for Grades 2–4:

I can:

- **Write a letter asking for a response**

- **Create a greeting card to send**

- **Write a postcard advocating for a cause I believe in**

- **Compose an email, giving my opinion about a topic**

- **Draft a tweet on an issue for my teacher to post**

Letter Writing station set up.

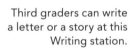

Third graders can write a letter or a story at this Writing station.

Resources

You will want students to write a variety of texts for different purposes at the Writing station throughout the year. Change what they might write periodically, based on what you've been teaching your class to do as writers. Avoid the temptation to just throw in "cute writing stuff" for fun. Instead, think about what you've taught well that you want students to continue practicing at the Writing station.

Two simple ways to keep your Writing station fresh and interesting are to use word banks and seasonal writing. Word banks will help students expand their vocabulary and get started with their writing. (One school I worked with told me that the simple addition of a few word banks with teachers modeling improved the Writing station more than anything else they'd tried!) And just as advertisers use the seasons to promote buying, you can use seasons to promote writing!

Word Banks for the Writing Station

Keep these simple. Brainstorm a short list of words that match a topic. Add illustrations so *all* students can read and use the words. Pay attention to what your students are interested in as you create word banks. Ask them for their ideas of topics.

Another idea is to glue a photo kids might be interested in onto white paper and add a related word bank created with your class. Model how to use a word bank in your own writing before moving it to the Writing station. You can find printable Grades K–1 word banks online at **resources.corwin.com/ simplystations-writing**.

Here are some topics to get you started:

- Foods kids like (e.g., *pizza, tacos, spaghetti*)

- Places kids like to go (use logos from restaurants, stores, and local places they know)

- Family members (e.g., *mom, dad, sister, brother, aunt, uncle, cousin, grandma, grandpa*)

- Things kids do at recess (e.g., *playground, recess, swings, sliding board, ball*)

- Topics related to what you're studying in science or social studies (e.g., *community, citizenship, space, weather*)

- Things related to popular or traditional culture (e.g., *superheroes, cartoon characters, pow wows, hip hop*)

Writing word banks at the Writing station are vocabulary and spelling resources.

Word banks built with photos of things kids are interested in posted at the Writing station. Lakota words are included at this Native American school.

Seasonal Writing Ideas

You might make lists of seasonal words to use as word banks, too. Place these at the Writing station after you've made them with your class and modeled with them during writing time.

Here are a few ideas for writing that are based on the seasons:

SEASON	FOCUS	KINDS OF WRITING TO DO
Fall	• Back to school • Fall leaves • Shorter days • Halloween • Thanksgiving	• Letters to your family • Informational text about fall • Stories/narratives about summertime • Scary stories, lists of costumes or treats, poems • Gratitude journal
Winter	• Winter holidays • New Year/new beginnings • Snow, colder weather • Valentine's Day	• Wish lists, thank you letters • Goal setting, times you tried new things • Poems or informational text, stories • Cards and love letters to family or friends
Spring	• Nature (signs of spring) • Birds, flowers, trees • Rain, clouds • St. Patrick's Day	• Field guides or informational text • Poems, observations • Wishes you have, times you were lucky
Summer	• Swimming, boating, beach • Neighborhood • Juneteenth and 4th of July	• Procedural text of water safety rules • Narratives about your neighborhood • Advocate for change, family stories, compare and contrast these holidays

(Mostly) Free Digital Tools for Writing

Young children will learn to write with physical materials such as markers and paper, but they can still use technology to help them as writers. Older students will enjoy using digital tools as they write, too. I recommend that you choose just a few apps to use well and teach kids (and their parents) to use these. Start with ones your campus already has installed on your devices. Then let students choose the tools that best meet their needs. I've listed several digital writing tools I like (most of which are free) below:

For Planning:

- **http://www.readwritethink.org/classroom-resources/student-interactives/story-30008.html** This free digital story map tool from readwritethink.org (an NCTE site) allows kids to type in ideas as they plan a story. Each graphic organizer asks one question at a time. Kids choose from printable maps for characters, setting, conflict, and resolution. Good for older students.

- **http://www.readwritethink.org/classroom-resources/student-interactives/cube-creator-30850.html** Kids can plan to write by making a cube. There are four choices: bio, mystery, story, or create-your-own about a topic. It's a fun way for kids to think using question prompts to plan what they will write. It's good for older kids.

- **https://www.controlaltachieve.com/2017/09/build-jackolantern.html**

- **https://www.controlaltachieve.com/2017/11/turkey-templates.html**

- **https://www.controlaltachieve.com/2016/12/build-snowman.html** At this site, kids can use directions on Google Slides to build things (e.g., jack-o-lantern, turkey, and snowman) and then write about them. Building helps them think and plan.

For Writing Digital Books:

- **https://bookcreator.com** Book Creator is a simple tool for creating awesome digital books. Create your own teaching resources or have your students take the reins. (This is a subscription site.)

- **https://www.mystorybook.com** A simple program where kids have four choices to design their stories: items (characters, familiar objects), draw (drawing tools), text (text box to type in words), and scene (backgrounds). It's very easy to navigate and great for young writers.

For Editing:

- **https://www.dictionary.com/e/apps** This app can be used offline. Kids can look up spellings of words and use the thesaurus, too.

- **https://www.grammarly.com** A great tool for helping with language conventions, such as noun–verb agreement, spelling, and punctuation. Kids can type in their writing and have it checked.

For Sharing and Storing Writing:

- **https://padlet.com** Padlet is a virtual bulletin board where kids can share their writing.

- **https://web.seesaw.me** Seesaw is another app you might use for writing. Log in. Then go to the Community page, type in your grade level, and search activities for writing. I love that kids can use it easily and it can be shared with parents. Great home–school connections!

- **https://getrocketbook.com** The Rocketbook is a special notebook and free mobile app. Write in it with an erasable Pilot Frixion pen, and it is reusable by putting a drop of water on the page. It saves your work to the cloud, too. (Not free, but still very cool!)

- **https://www.wordclouds.com** Word clouds can be used after writing, especially informational text. Use them to check if the main ideas come across in your piece of writing.

Authors and Illustrators to Study

I recommend studying authors and illustrators to help students make connections between reading and writing. Learning about authors will help students apply what they learn to their own writing. It's interesting (and inspiring) to find out where authors get their ideas!

Following are some culturally diverse authors and illustrators I love. (I've included a similar list in *Simply Stations: Independent Reading*, too.) You might study a new author every four to six weeks. Share author interviews and information with your class. Then post a photo of the author with what you learned from them and encourage kids to try similar things. You might have kids use the author's craft cards you've taught with here, too. I've listed sites with information telling about the authors and their lives on the following pages.

KINDERGARTEN

AUTHOR	INTERESTING FACT	SITE TELLING ABOUT THE AUTHOR'S LIFE
Derrick Barnes	● First African American male to write greeting cards for Hallmark	https://thebrownbookshelf.com/28days/derrick-barnes/
Lois Ehlert	● Came from a family of makers ● Mom was a seamstress and dad a woodworker	https://www.readingrockets.org/books/interviews/ehlert
Denise Fleming	● Makes her own paper ● Likes being a hermit	http://www.kidlit411.com/2016/09/Kidlit411-Author-Illustrator-Denise-Fleming.html
Vashti Harrison	● Was a filmmaker ● Didn't want to write about boy legends, just girls at first	https://www.publishersweekly.com/pw/by-topic/childrens/childrens-authors/article/81771-four-questions-for-vashti-harrison.html
Salina Yoon	● Born in rural Korea ● Had no TV ● Moved to the United States at age four	http://www.salinayoon.com/About.html
David Shannon	● Writes about his life as a kid ● Does paintings over and over to get them right	https://www.youtube.com/watch?v=5eKLeIT7axg

AUTHOR	INTERESTING FACT	SITE TELLING ABOUT THE AUTHOR'S LIFE
Matt De La Peña and Christian Robinson	● Greatly respect family who came before them ● Matt's family is from Mexico ● Christian's grandmas who raised him are also from Mexico	https://www.youtube.com/watch?v=4vIPY-NKDSI https://www.publishersweekly.com/pw/by-topic/childrens/childrens-authors/article/78215-in-conversation-matt-de-la-pe-a-and-christian-robinson.html
Alma Flor Ada	● Her grandma in Cuba taught her to read by writing words on the earth with a stick	https://www.readingrockets.org/books/interviews/ada
Ezra Jack Keats	● Jewish man named Katz ● Changed his name in 1947 due to anti-Semitism ● Wrote about Peter, a Black boy inspired by a photo from *Life* magazine, because there weren't books about children of color	https://www.ezra-jack-keats.org/ezras-life/ https://coloursofus.com/author-spotlight-ezra-jack-keats/
Margaree King Mitchell	● Wrote a story about a Black grandfather because she couldn't find one in the library to read to her son	https://thebrownbookshelf.com/28days/day-28-margaree-king-mitchell/
Duncan Tonatiuh	● Grew up in Mexico ● Uses ancient Mexican art as his inspiration with a contemporary twist	https://www.youtube.com/watch?v=Ti7aMU1xRyc https://www.youtube.com/watch?v=n7-kzJVcOUw

(Continued)

(Continued)

AUTHOR	INTERESTING FACT	SITE TELLING ABOUT THE AUTHOR'S LIFE
Jacqueline Woodson	• Her mom was a civil rights activist • Her great-great-grandparents were part of the Underground Railroad	https://www.jacquelinewoodson.com/ https://www.youtube.com/watch?v=KfGBtIG6CgM
S.D. Nelson	• Paints on animal skins and bone • Member of the Sioux from the Dakotas	https://www.sdnelson.net/about/

GRADES 3–4

AUTHOR	INTERESTING FACT	SITE TELLING ABOUT THE AUTHOR'S LIFE
Lenore Look	• Began publishing her own books in first grade and sold them to her friends	https://thestylinglibrarian.wordpress.com/2012/10/26/styling-librarian-author-interview-lenore-look/ https://www.penguinrandomhouse.com/authors/73006/lenore-look
Pam Muñoz Ryan	• Wrote down stories about her grandparents' childhood	http://www.judynewmanatscholastic.com/blog/2019/09/author-interview-pam-munoz-ryan-esperanza-rising/ https://www.btsb.com/2014/07/10/pam-munoz-ryan-about-the-author/
Joseph Bruchac	• His family is Abenaki • He says to write what you know	https://www.scholastic.com/teachers/articles/teaching-content/joseph-bruchac-interview-transcript/

AUTHOR	INTERESTING FACT	SITE TELLING ABOUT THE AUTHOR'S LIFE
Jeff Kinney	• Tried unsuccessfully to get a cartoon syndicated	https://wimpykid.com/about-the-author/ https://www.youtube.com/watch?v=Idc0_OerBrA
Erin Entrada Kelly	• Filipino–American who grew up feeling like she didn't fit in	https://www.readingrockets.org/books/interviews/entrada-kelly https://www.publishersweekly.com/pw/by-topic/childrens/childrens-authors/article/76377-q-a-with-erin-entrada-kelly.html
Walter Dean Myers	• Had speech problems growing up	https://www.scholastic.com/teachers/videos/teaching-content/walter-dean-myers-interview-myers-beauty-language/ https://walterdeanmyers.net/about/
Dav Pilkey	• When he worked at a pizza place, they spelled his name, Dave, wrong, and it stuck	https://www.readingrockets.org/books/interviews/pilkey https://pilkey.com/author

Picture Books to Introduce Writing Conventions

You might use a picture book or two to introduce a writing convention you'll be focusing on. This is a fun way to get kids to think about the concept and why it's important. Here are some titles to get you started. These can be used across grade levels, but look at the books carefully to be sure it matches the age and stage of what you'll be teaching your students to do!

CAPITALIZATION	PUNCTUATION	SPELLING	LANGUAGE CONVENTIONS
• *The Case of the Incapacitated Capitals* by Robin Pulver	• *If You Were an Apostrophe* by Shelly Lyons • *Punctuation Takes a Vacation* by Robin Pulver • *Punctuation Celebration* by Elsa Knight Bruno • *Yo? Yes!* by Chris Raschka	• *The Spelling Bee before Recess* by Deborah Lee Rose • *If You're So Smart, How Come You Can't Spell Mississippi?* by Barbara Esham • *An Inconvenient Alphabet* by Beth Anderson • *The Infinity Year of Avalon James* by Dana Middleton • *Lexie the Word Wrangler* by Rebecca Van Slyke	• *Nouns and Verbs Have a Field Day* by Robin Pulver • *It's Hard to Be a Verb* by Julia Cook • *If You Were a Conjunction* by Nancy Loewen • Ruth Heller books • Brian P. Cleary books

Picture Books to Introduce Writing Genres

Here are some picture books to read aloud to introduce several types of writing children may be doing in kindergarten through fourth grade. This is not an exhaustive list, just some books to get your started. (For opinion writing specific titles, check out pages 120–122.) Please add to these titles as you find new books!

NARRATIVES/ STORIES	INFORMATIONAL TEXT SERIES	JOURNALS OR DIARIES	CORRESPONDENCE
• *Little Red Writing* by Joan Holub	• National Geographic Kids Readers	• *Diary of a Wimpy Kid* by Jeff Kinney	• *Dear Mr. Blueberry* by Simon James
• *Idea Jar* by Adam Lehrhaupt	• I Can Read! series from HarperCollins	• *Diary of a Worm* by Doreen Cronin	• *Dear Mrs. LaRue* by Mark Teague
• *This Is a Good Story* by Adam Lehrhaupt	• Books by Gail Gibbons or Seymour Simon	• *Owl Diaries* by Rebecca Elliott	• *Can I Be Your Dog?* by Troy Cummings
• *A Squiggly Story* by Andrew Larsen	• Let's Read and Find Out series from HarperCollins	• *Diary of a Minecraft Zombie* by Zach Zombie	• *A Letter to Amy* by Ezra Jack Keats
• *Ralph Tells a Story* by Abby Hanlon	• True Books from Children's Press	• *Amelia's Notebook* by Marissa Moss	• *The Day the Crayons Quit* by Drew Daywalt
• *Rocket Writes a Story* by Tad Hills	• I Wonder Why series from Kingfisher	• *Dork Diaries* by Rachel Renée Russell	• *Ten Thank-You Letters* by Daniel Kirk
• *How to Write a Story* by Kate Messner	• Who Was? series from Grosset & Dunlap	• *Harriet's Monster Diary* by Raun Melmed	• *A Letter to My Teacher* by Deborah Hopkinson
• *Stella Tells Her Story* by Janiel Wagstaff	• What If You Had? series by Sandra Markle	• *Like the Willow Tree* (Dear America series) by Lois Lowry	• *The Jolly Postman* by Allan Ahlberg
			• *Dear Juno* by Soyung Pak
			• *Stringbean's Trip to the Shining Sea* by Vera B. Williams
			• *Abuela's Special Letters* by Jacqueline Jules
			• *I Wrote You a Note* by Lizi Boyd

BIBLIOGRAPHY OF TEXTS USED IN LESSONS

TEXT USED IN SAMPLE MODEL LESSONS	STANDARD AND GRADE LEVELS	PAGE NUMBER OF THE LESSON
Dotlich, R. K. (2015). *One Day, The End: Short, Very Short, Shorter-Than-Ever Stories*. Honesdale, PA: Boyds Mills Press.	TS2 Primary	83
Dunklee, A. (2011). *My Name Is Elizabeth*. Toronto: Kids Can Press.	TS5 Primary	145
Hanlon, A. (2011). *Ralph Tells a Story*. New York: Two Lions	TS1 Primary	66
Messier, M. (2016). *The Branch*. Toronto: Kids Can Press.	TS5 Intermediate	148
National Geographic. (2019, April 4). "Three Notable African-American Inventors of the 18th Century." Retrieved July 1, 2020 from https://newsela.com/read/natgeo-elem-african-american-inventors/id/44816	TS3 Intermediate	107
Portis, A. (2019). *Hey, Water!* New York: Neal Porter Books.	TS3 Primary	102
Spinelli, E. (2008). *The Best Story*. New York: Dial Books.	TS2 Intermediate	86
Stead, T. (2014). *What Is the Best Pet?* Mankato, MN: Capstone Classroom.	TS4 Primary	127
Wagstaff, J. (2018). *Stella Writes an Opinion*. New York: Scholastic Teaching Resources.	TS4 Intermediate	131
Wong, J. S. (2002). *You Have to Write*. New York: Margaret K. McElderry Books.	TS1 Intermediate	68

Because...
ALL TEACHERS ARE LEADERS

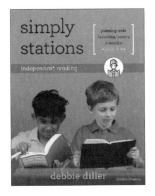
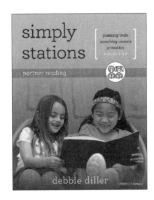
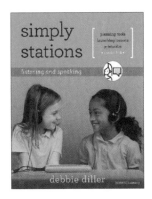

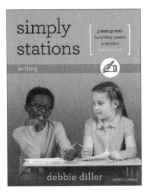
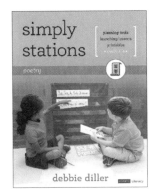
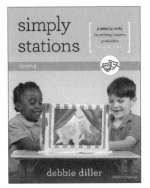

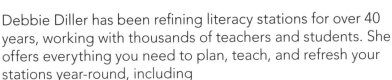

Debbie Diller has been refining literacy stations for over 40 years, working with thousands of teachers and students. She offers everything you need to plan, teach, and refresh your stations year-round, including

- Step-by-step instructions for launching and maintaining the station;

- Whole group lesson plans, based on key literacy standards, to introduce and support partner work;

- Printable teacher and student tools;

- On-the-spot assessment ideas and troubleshooting tips;

- Lists of grade-level specific materials; and

- Real-classroom photos so you see the possibilities firsthand.

Don't miss the other books in the Simply Stations series!

- Simply Stations: Word Study

- Simply Stations: Let's Talk

- Simply Stations: Inquiry and Research

To learn more, visit corwin.com/simplystations

CORWIN

A SAGE Publishing Company

Helping educators make the greatest impact

CORWIN HAS ONE MISSION: to enhance education through intentional professional learning.

We build long-term relationships with our authors, educators, clients, and associations who partner with us to develop and continuously improve the best evidence-based practices that establish and support lifelong learning.